QUARTET

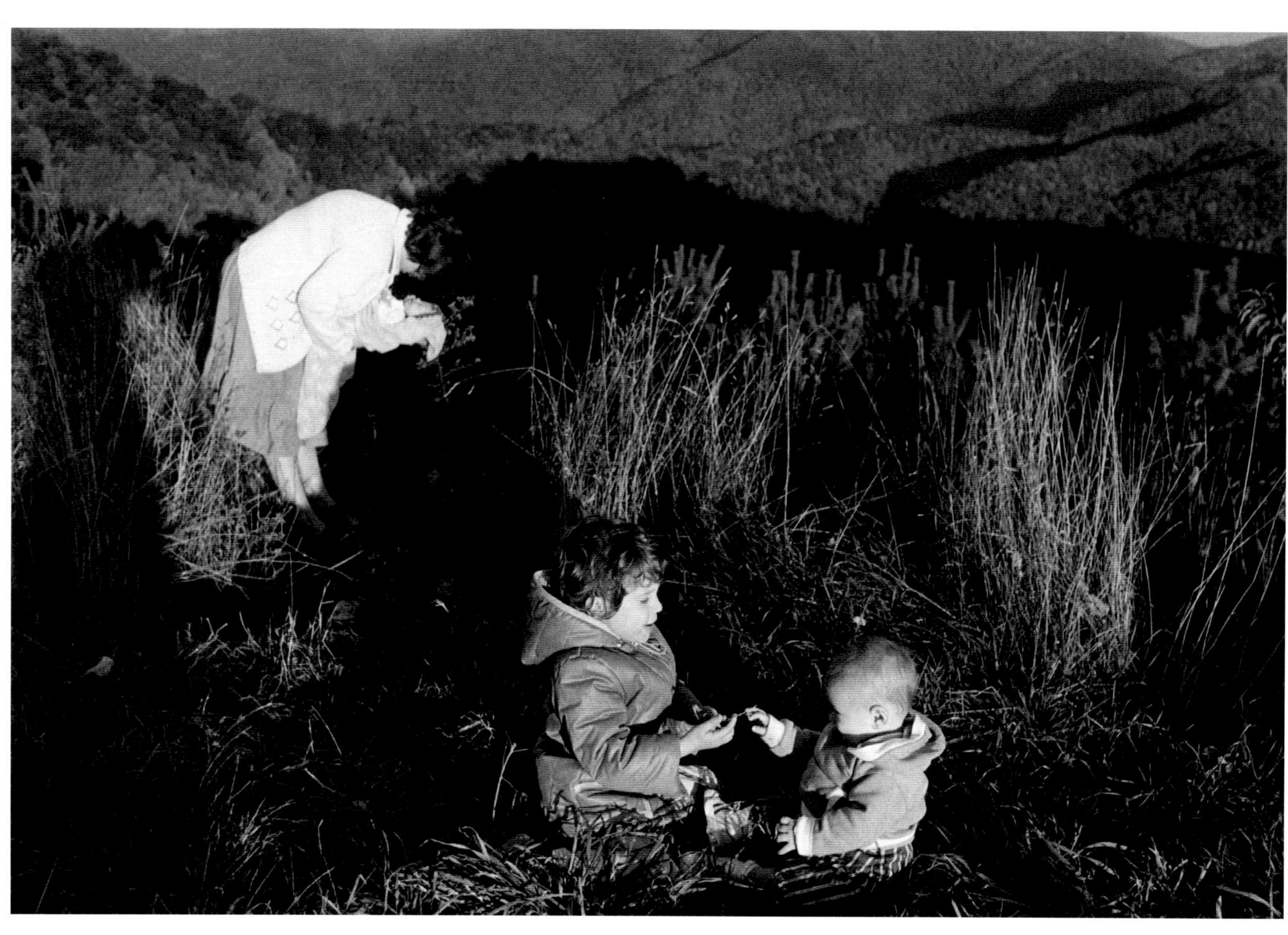

QUARTET

· Four North Carolina Photographers ·

Rob Amberg
Caroline Vaughan
Elizabeth Matheson
John Rosenthal

Introduction by Georgann Eubanks

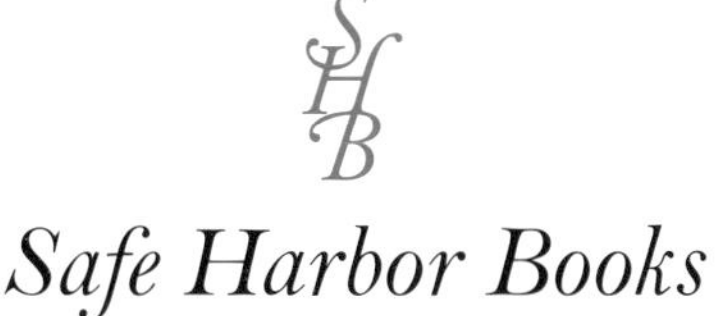

Safe Harbor Books

NEW LONDON · NEW HAMPSHIRE
ASHEVILLE · NORTH CAROLINA

QUARTET
is published in honor of
Herschel and Eleanor Ponder

Additional financial support comes from the
Confluence Company,
Asheville, North Carolina

FRONTISPIECE:

On Troublesome Gap

Madison County, North Carolina

Introduction by Georgann Eubanks

It's no secret that sales of films, chemicals, and traditional photographic papers are in decline. Instead, we witness the world through digital media that can be instantly manipulated to show anything the imagination contrives. Video images rocket across the television screen at thirty frames per second. We find ourselves in the hands of young artists hell-bent on heightening our human capacity to endure this relentless battery of scenes and special effects. How fast and how much can you take in? they seem to ask.

In this context, *Quartet* is a throwback, an endangered art form. Yet this collection of thirty-four images from four gifted North Carolina photographers of the same generation is refreshing in the quiet pace required to absorb them. Such a contemplative venture is the same process that these prints required of their makers: a slow dance in near dark.

Rob Amberg, the first photographer represented here, has chosen to live and work in a North Carolina mountain county that languishes behind the times—arguably because its steep terrain has always been so confining. The prolific North Carolina novelist Manly Wade Wellman once wrote of Madison County: "Its few towns and settlements are so small among the soaring crests and deep-plunging hollows, where roads wriggle their way like snakes. You can't get into Madison County save through a gap."

For years now Amberg has navigated these deep gaps and immersed himself in the community to photograph his neighbors—hardscrabble folks who live close to the land. Occasionally he ventures to other rural communities in the South where agrarian traditions still dominate. The images collected here demonstrate the connection between Amberg's subjects and the products of their labors: The side-lit chickens are echoed in the ghostly shape of their keeper. Mrs. Douglas's heavy-leafed collards seem to cast shadows across her entire yard and house in the same way that collard sales dominate the South Carolina countryside come New Year's. Carter Cosby's segregated melons make us wonder just what passage of scripture might be resting open on his belly.

Amberg's work is finally about preservation. He is securing images of practices that are being lost in the steady diminishment of rural life and replaced by our homogenized Wal-Mart culture.

But there is no sentimentality here—even the carnival that comes once a year to an island in the French Broad River seems tired and worn.

For her part, Caroline Vaughan has spent some thirty years carefully composing portraits of people and landscapes that work on the viewer at several levels. Vaughan often speaks in metaphor because she sees in metaphor. The details she fixes on in a landscape usually suggest human features and forms that are charged with sexual energy. Vaughan says that she always seeks out the most transient elements in a landscape, "things that took a shorter time to be created and that require non-discovery by humans to survive, like the mud dauber's nest. These fragile things I try to photograph in the most noninvasive ways," she says.

At least once a year over two decades, Vaughan made a series of portraits of her father, a skilled woodworker. This longitudinal study demonstrates the fine patina of human aging, sturdy and burnished as the oak cane that William Vaughan refused to carry for walking but used to steady his hands for his daughter's camera. Indeed, all of Caroline Vaughan's work aims to freeze time in order to distill its effects. The accumulation of slow moments—whether water coursing over stones or the slow pull of gravity on skin—is her preoccupation, an effort perhaps to anticipate grief and loss as a means to lessen their inevitable arrival.

Hillsborough-born Elizabeth Matheson offers a different twist on portraiture. As in a good short story, where what the author leaves out is as significant as what she puts in, Matheson shows us room after room from which the occupants have apparently just stepped away for a few minutes. We are left to ponder who they are and what they might have been doing, aided only by the angle of light, the formality of the furnishings, photos set out on a bureau, a door left ajar, an empty mirror.

In this small sampling of Matheson's work—which has, over the years, included important documentation of North Carolina's historic architecture—the contrast between the flowing interiors and the rigidly geometrical exteriors is haunting. Matheson's printing skills deliver a remarkable range of light and detail. "The light-filled stillness in Matheson's work is both engaging and somehow comforting," says Charlotte Vestal Brown, director of the Gallery of Art and Design at North Carolina State University. "I am always finding new things in her images, quirky things that I had not seen before. Elizabeth Matheson brings a passionate detachment to her work that is well mannered. You are always politely invited in." Matheson's genteel upbringing is inescapable in these elegant photographs.

John Rosenthal—public intellectual, scholar of English literature, and radio commentator as well as photographer—entices us to imagine the narrative line in his photographs, a story he captures in medias res. Rosenthal looks for the moment, the action that suggests what he has called "the active sensuality of the world itself, the whirling and jumping world."

Writing in the state-sponsored publication *NC Arts*, Rosenthal explains: "If photography is about anything, it is the deep surprise of living in the ordinary world. By virtue of walking through the fields and streets of this planet, focusing on the small and the unexpected, conferring attention on the helter-skelter juxtapositions of time and space, the photographer reminds us that the actual world is full of surprise, which is precisely what most people, imprisoned in habit and devoted to the familiar, tend to forget."

Rosenthal is true to his intentions. In these photographs, it is the juxtaposition of odd elements that creates the vivid moment which demands another look and then another: his son John Keats standing on a chair to embrace the fog in a field; the white cat twisting her body among new cornstalks; the placid girl and snarling dogs on a dirt road. Rosenthal's work is wry and urbane, a sensibility informed by the many years he has spent photographing in Manhattan. But here, when he turns his attention to more rural settings, the images still carry the unmistakable imprint of Rosenthal's narrative urge to show us the folly of the living—by turns dark and funny, but always compressed, reminiscent of the stories of Raymond Carver.

Ultimately, *Quartet*'s publisher Christopher Brookhouse and designer Dean Bornstein have selected images from these photographers that hum with subtle harmonies, each photographer adding another dimension to the resonant chord, all reminding us that against the din of digital media, there is yet a place for still images and deeper reflection. As John Rosenthal once explained to the *Independent Weekly*, "If there's an overriding need I feel, it's to slow things down," he said. "I can't imagine that there's any truth or beauty in the acceleration that seems to be the point of everything today." Caroline Vaughan said much the same of her effort: "I choose to make still images to slow the world I see. Only in this way can I filter the many layers down to a rhythm slow enough that I can maintain my balance. I stop time to make a fiction of stopping time."

The finely felt adagio playing here reminds us of a world that is rushing away. We can only hope that the art form as practiced by this quartet will somehow be sustained.

Georgann Eubanks is director of the
Duke University Writers' Workshop and co-owner of
Minnow Media, a documentary video firm in
Carrboro, North Carolina.

QUARTET

Rob Amberg

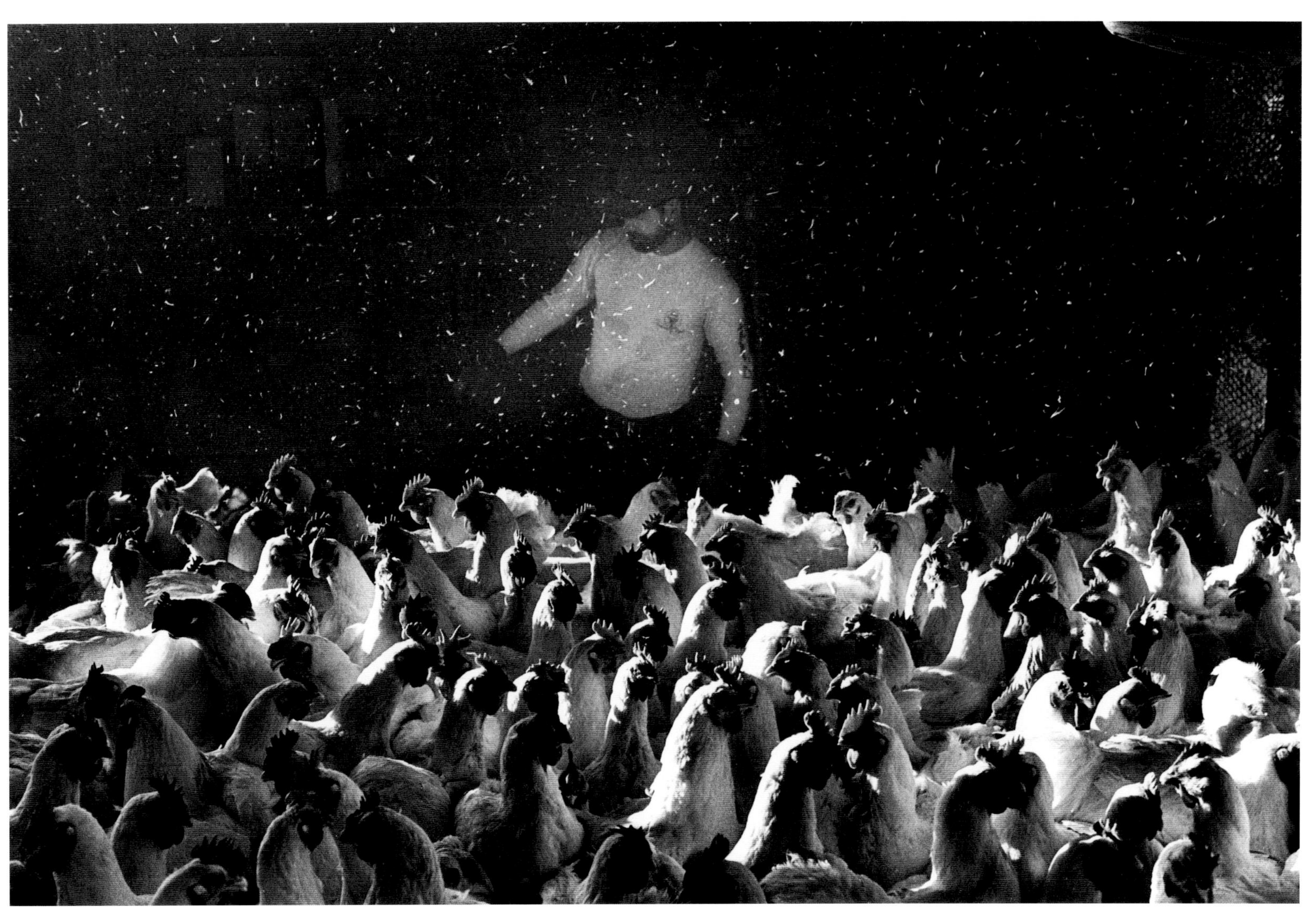

Chickencatcher
Chatham County, North Carolina

Mrs. Douglas and Her Collards
Columbia, South Carolina

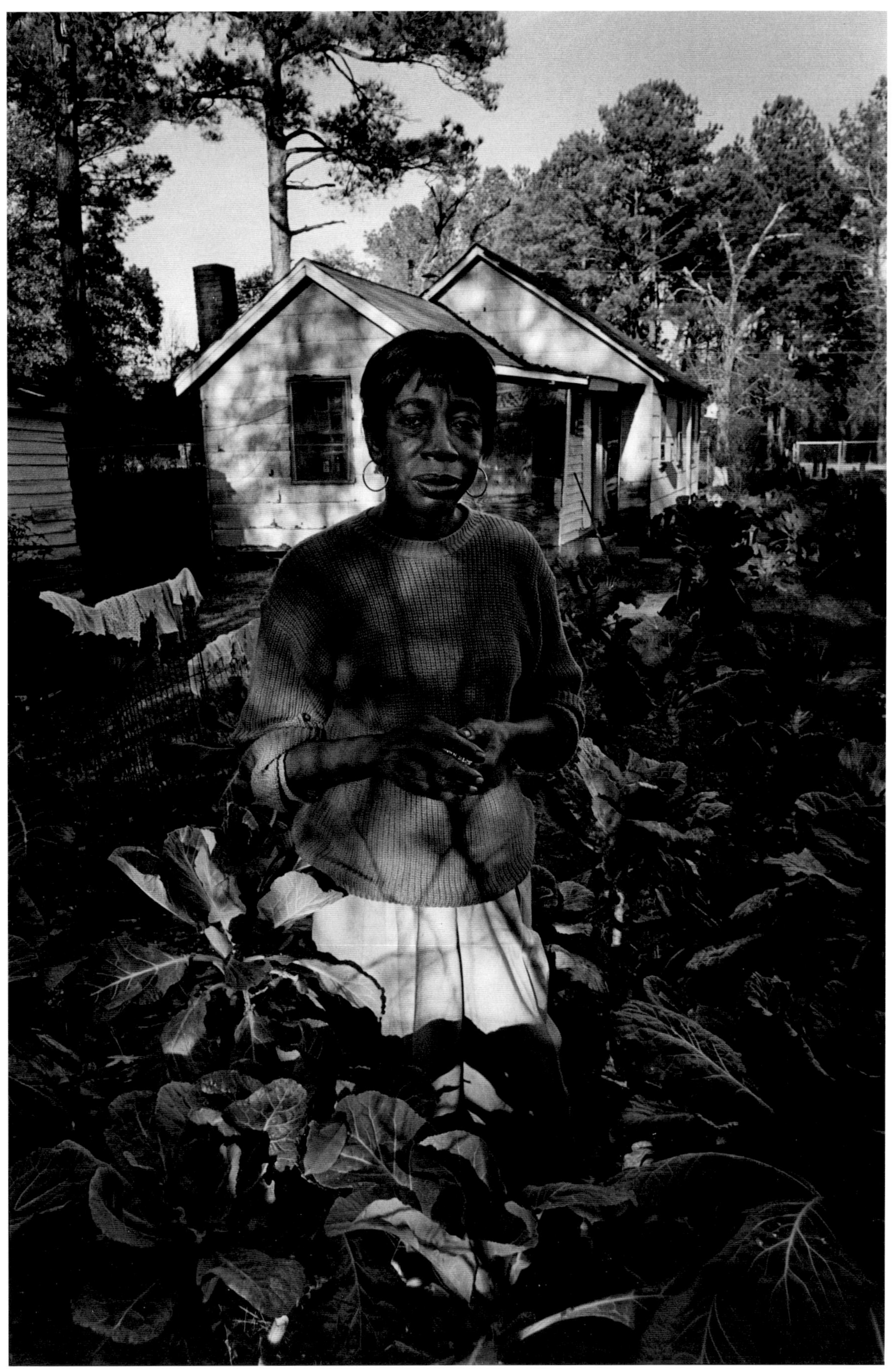

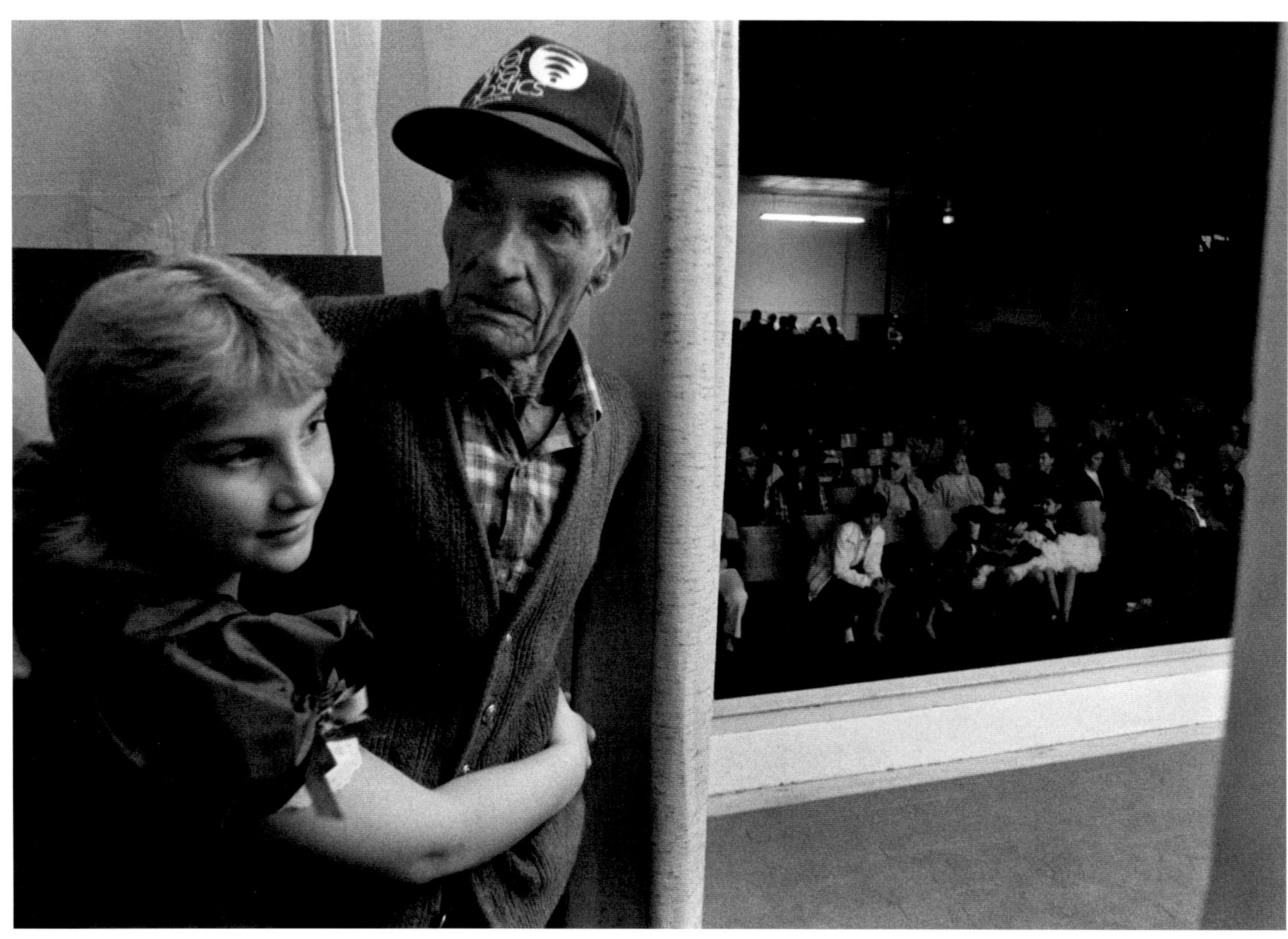

At the Democratic Party Fish Fry, Marshall
Madison County, North Carolina

Carnival on the Island, Marshall
Madison County, North Carolina

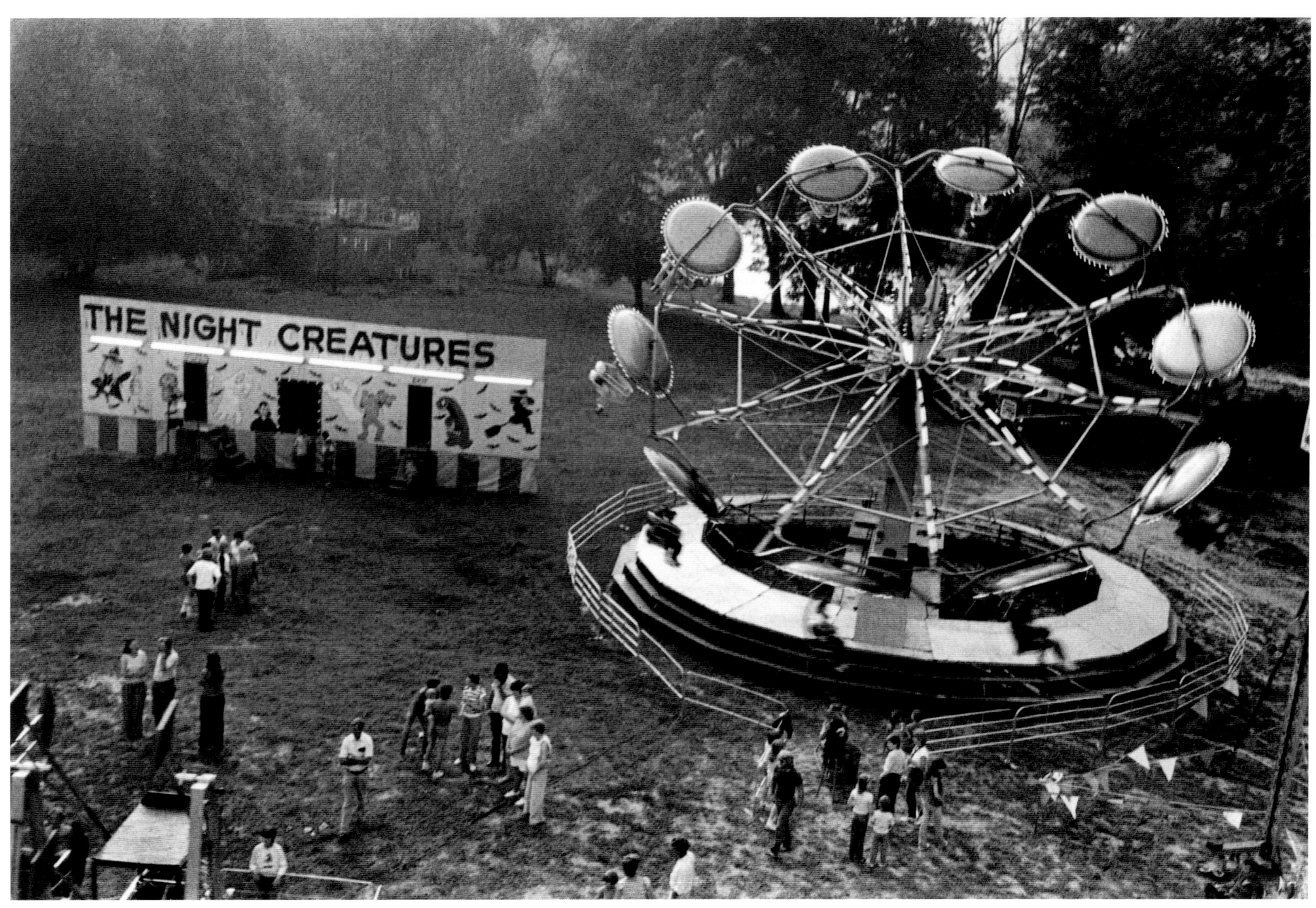

THE NIGHT CREATURES

Carter Cosby, Highway 24 South
Clinton, North Carolina

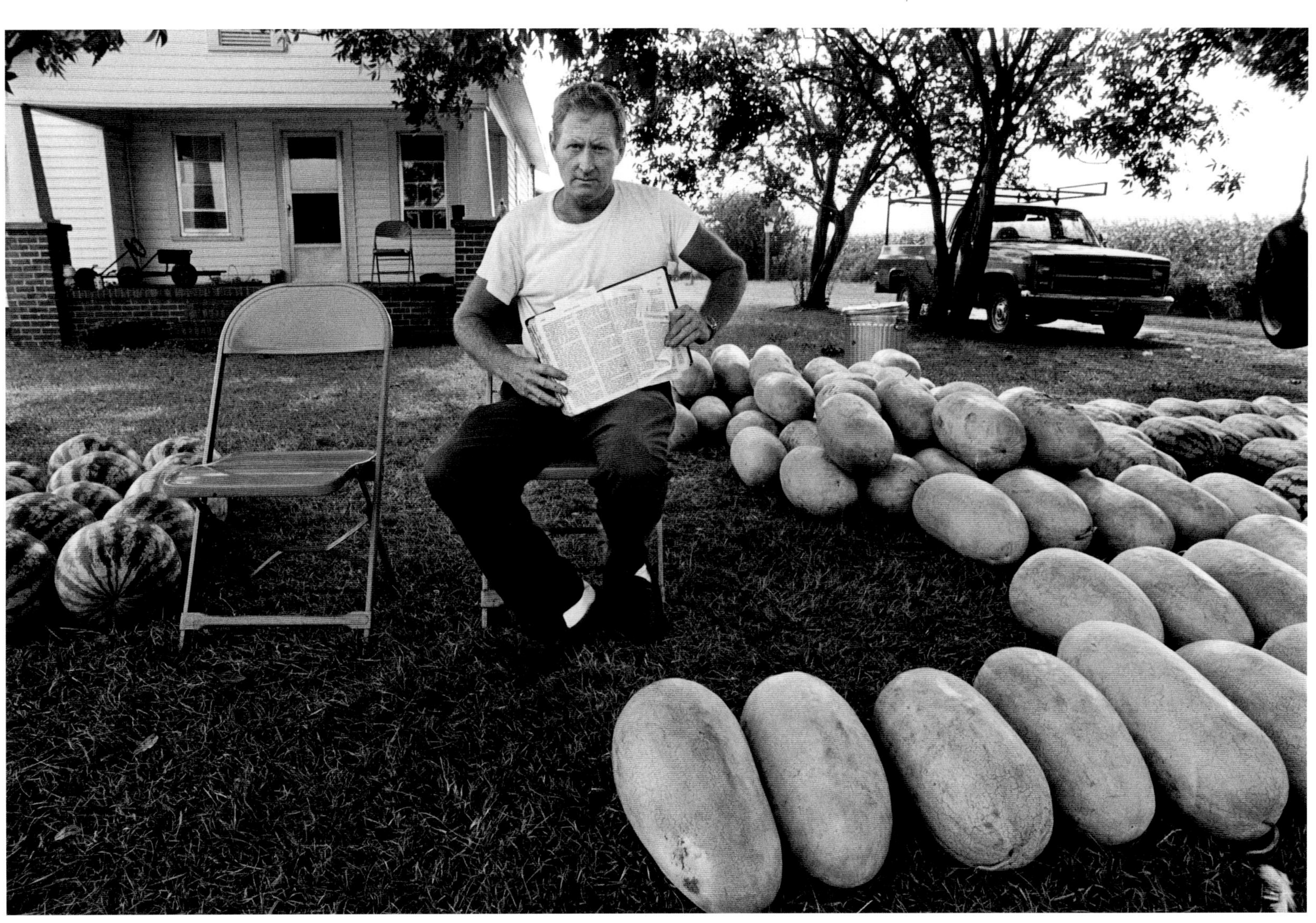

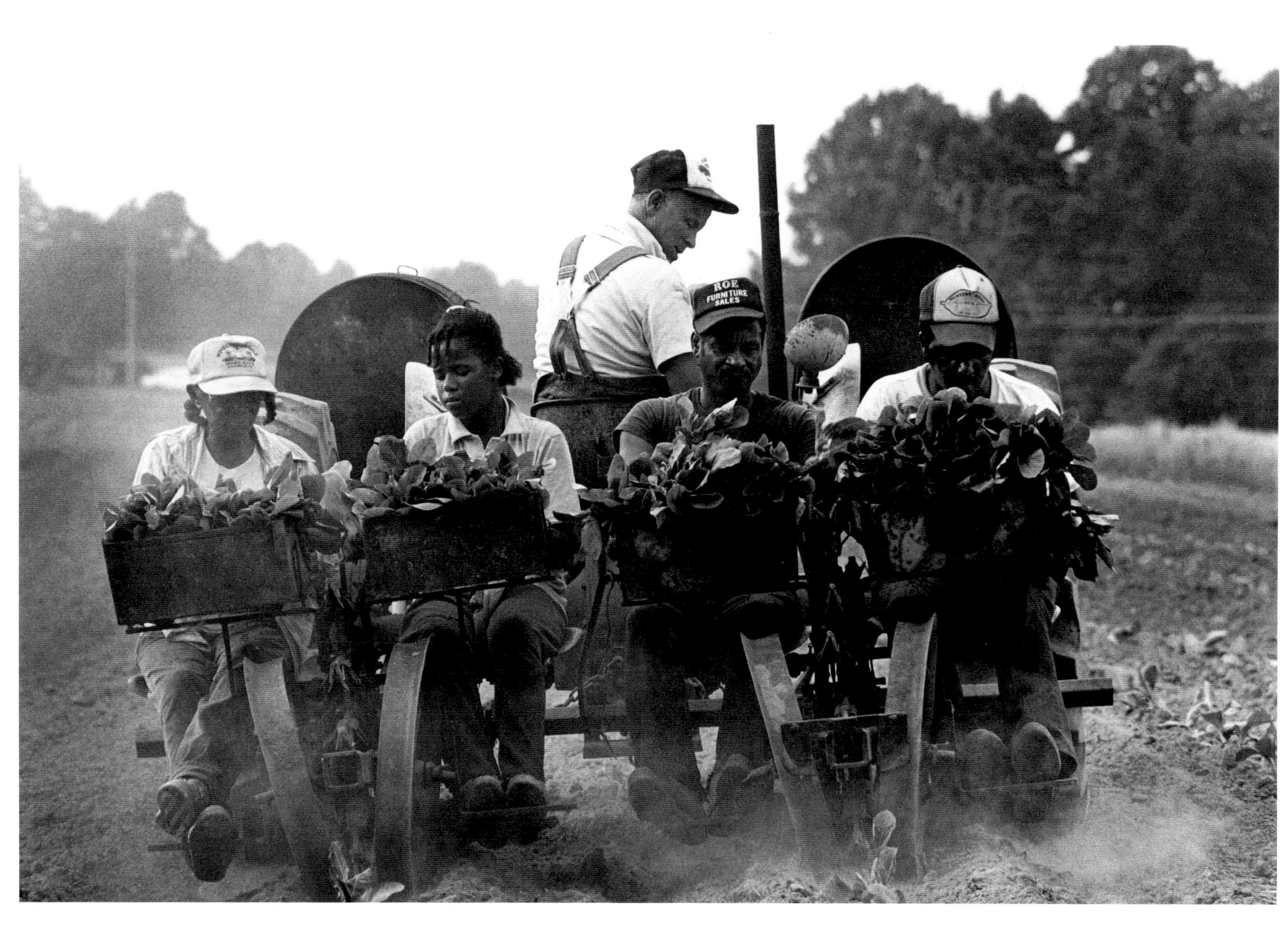

Jim Smyre and Family Setting Tobacco, Harmony

Iredell County, North Carolina

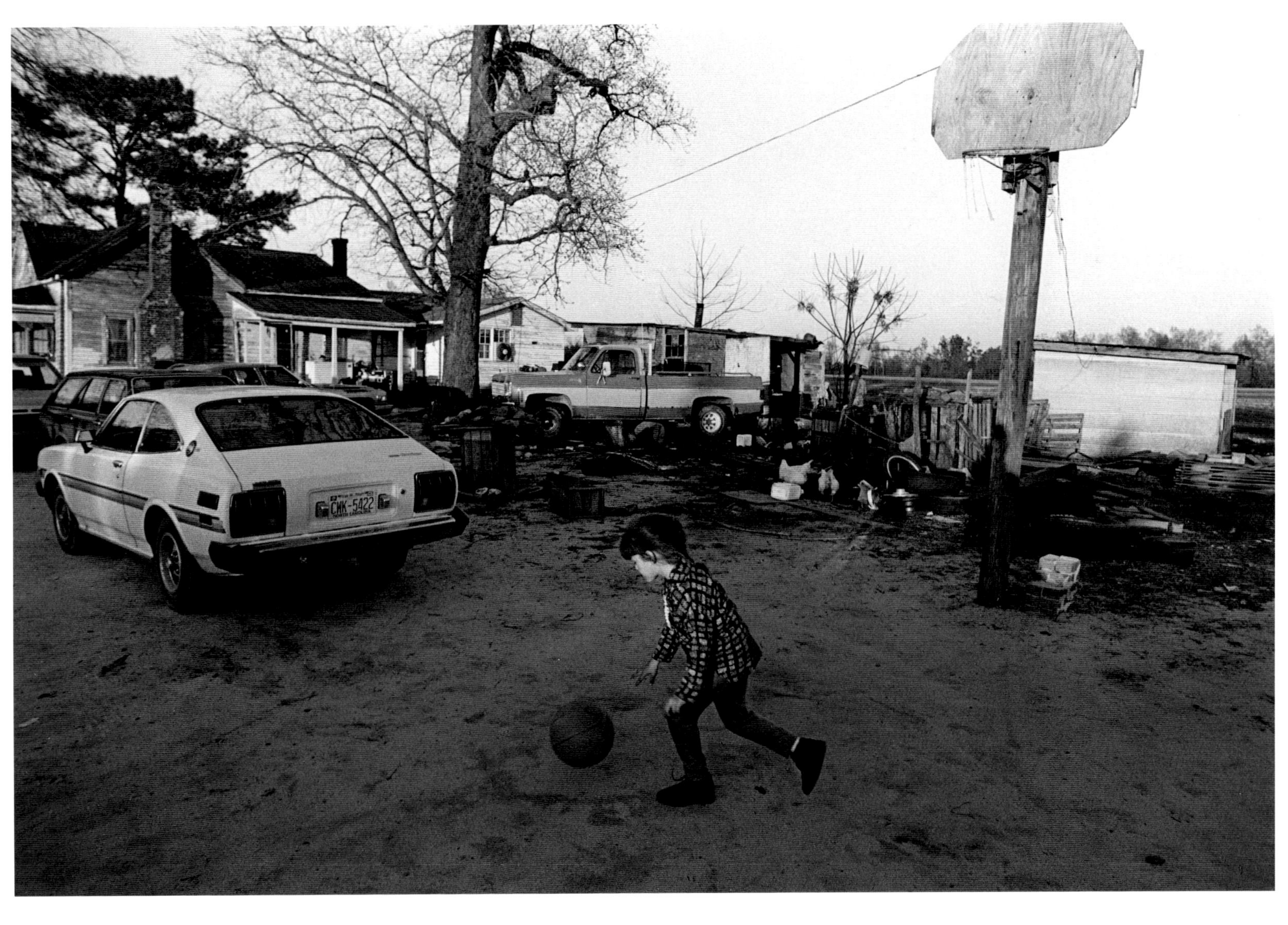

Sylvester Walker's Granddaughter Playing Basketball in the Front Yard
Spivey's Corner, North Carolina

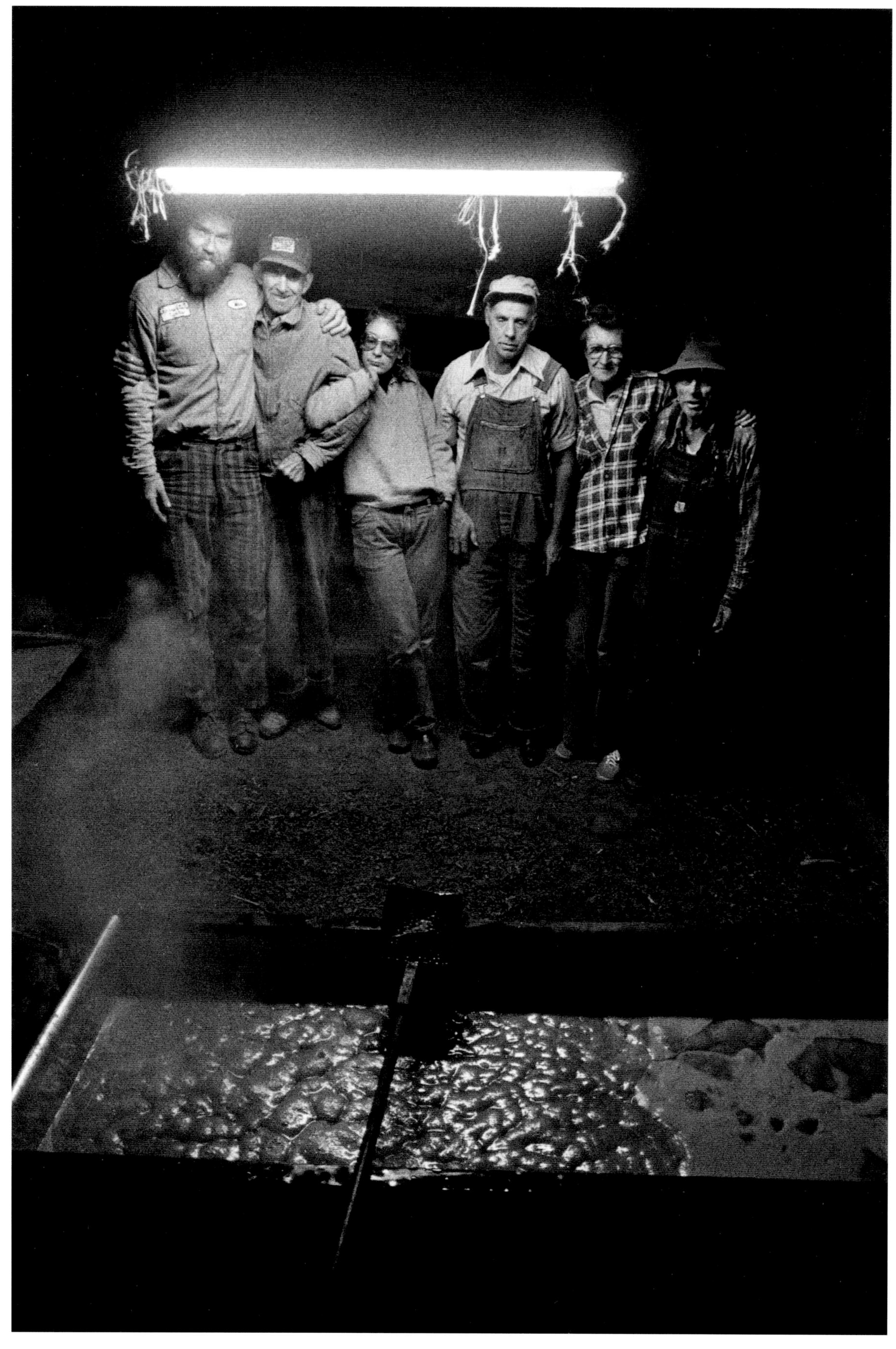

Molasses Making at Eldon Henderson's, Big Pine
Madison County, North Carolina

Caroline Vaughan

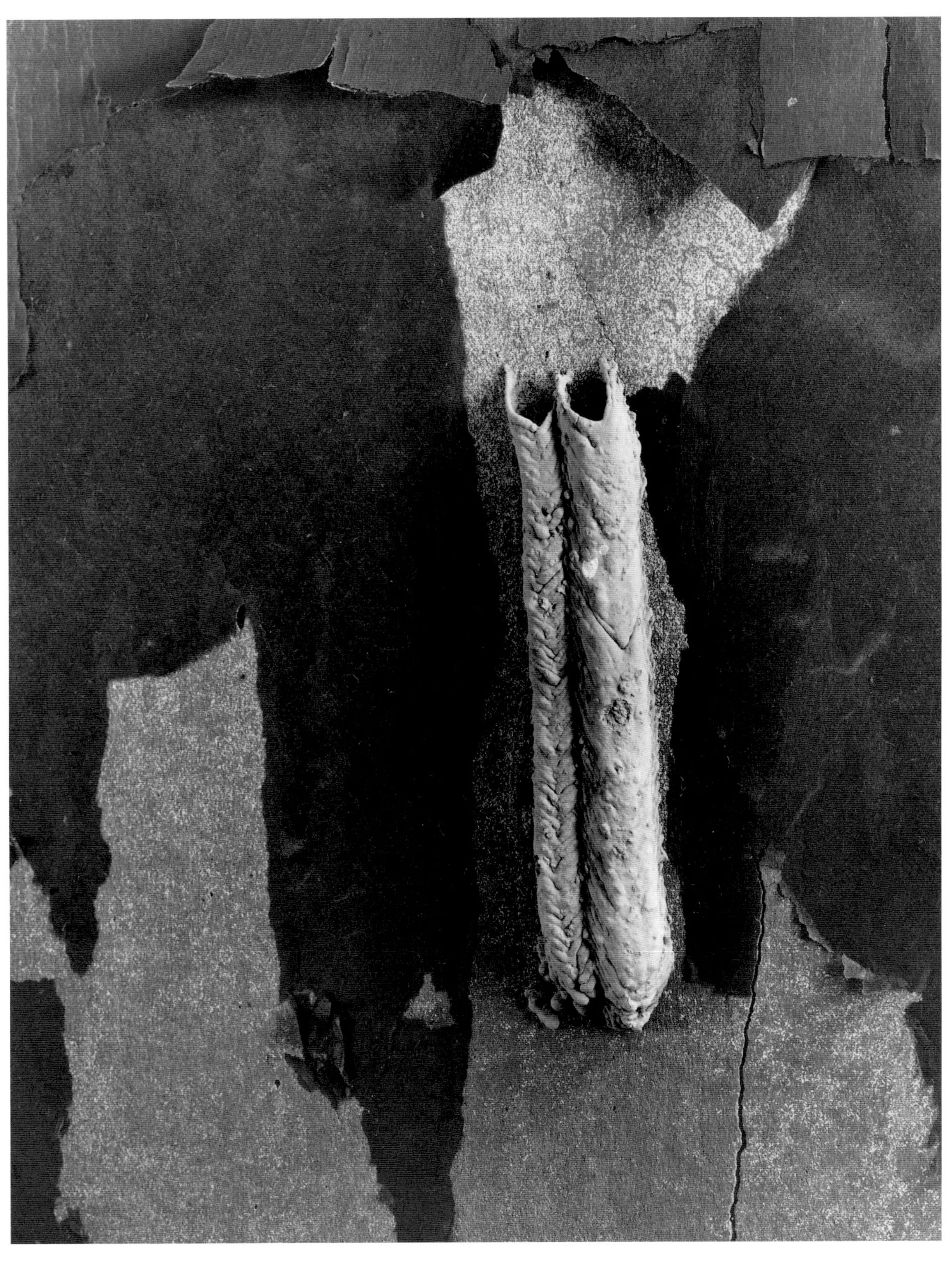

Mud Dauber Nest

Charlotte, North Carolina

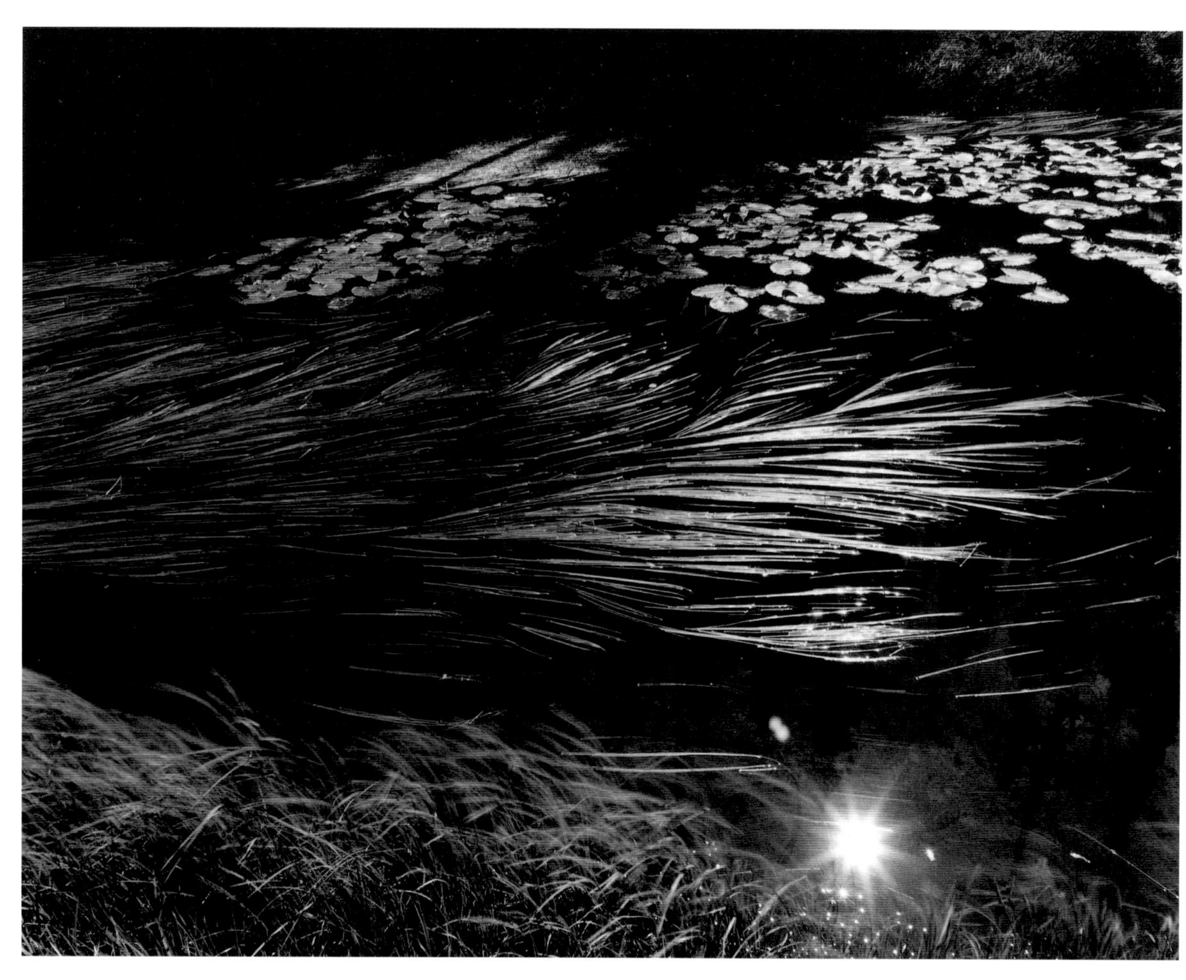

Continental Divide
Isa Lake, Wyoming

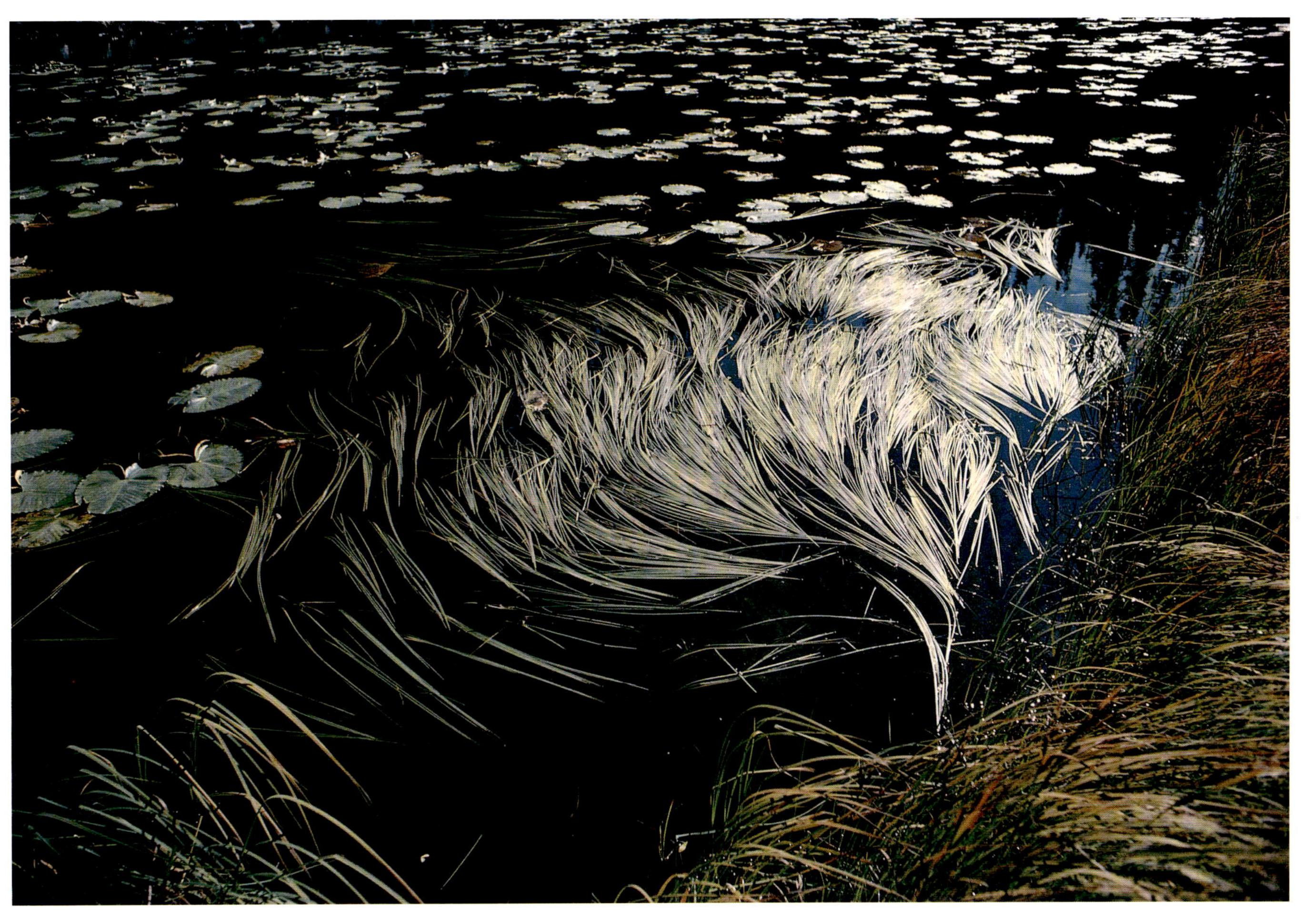

Continental Divide

Isa Lake, Wyoming

Yin Pond

Shackleford Island, North Carolina

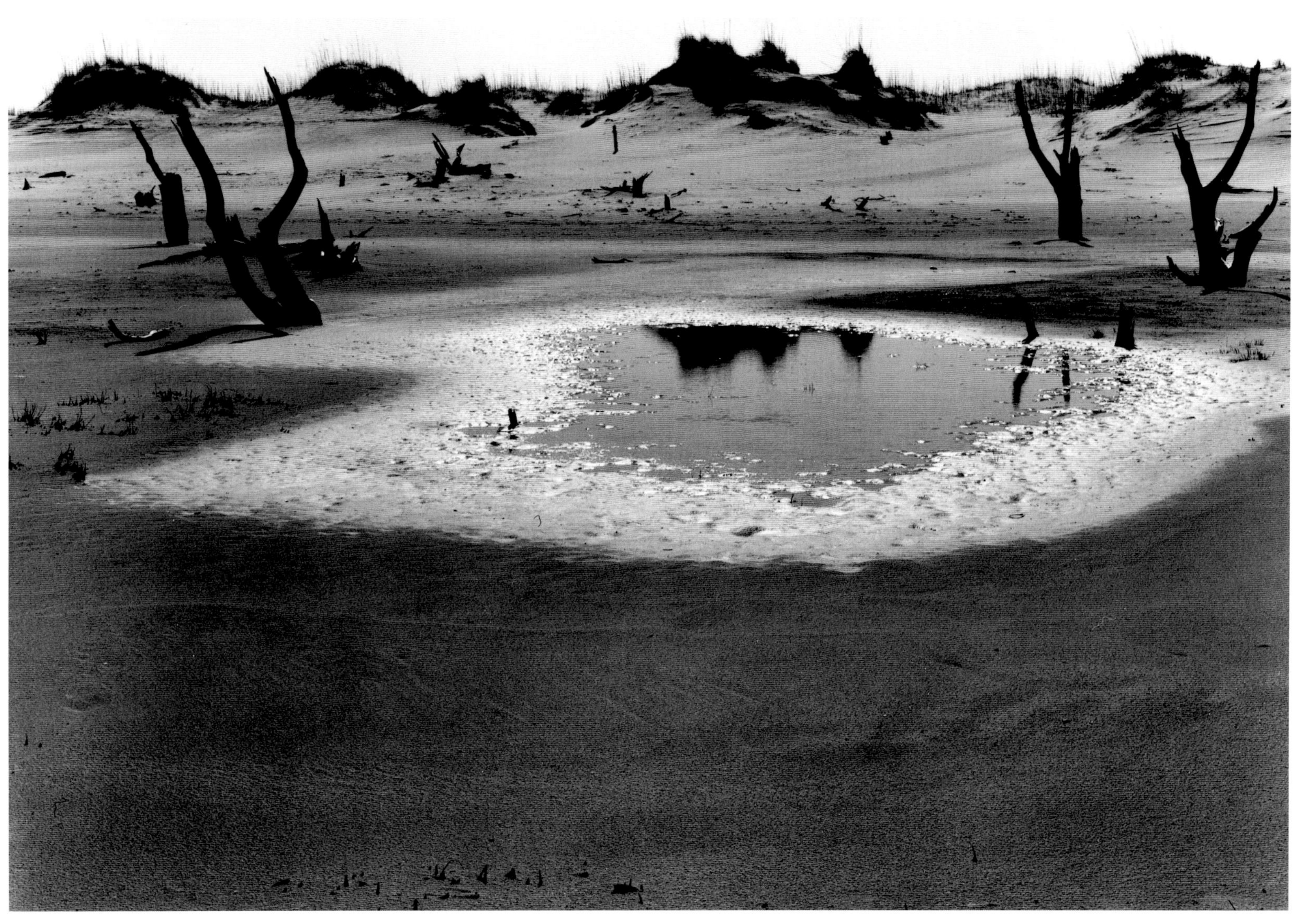

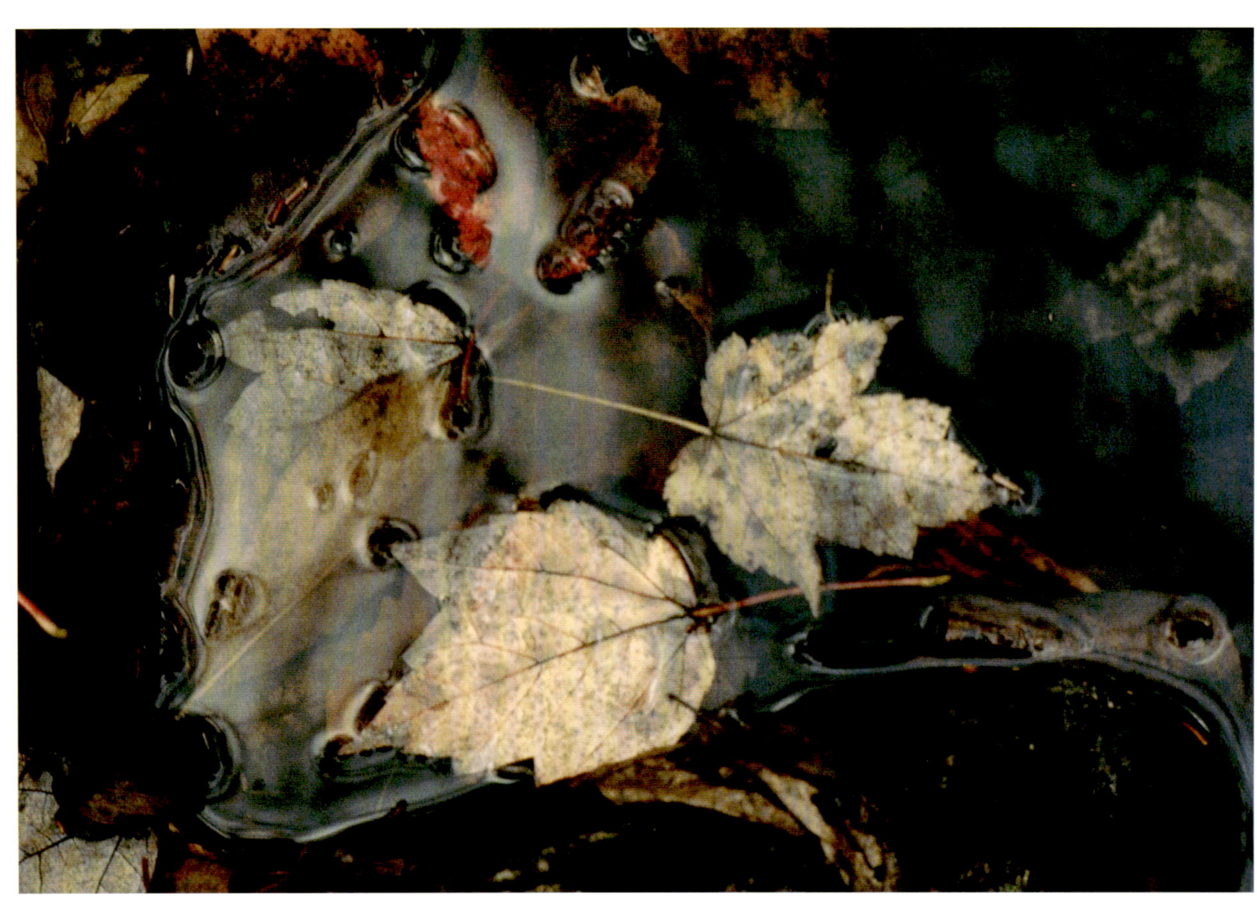

Leaves
North Carolina

Smokey Mountains

North Carolina

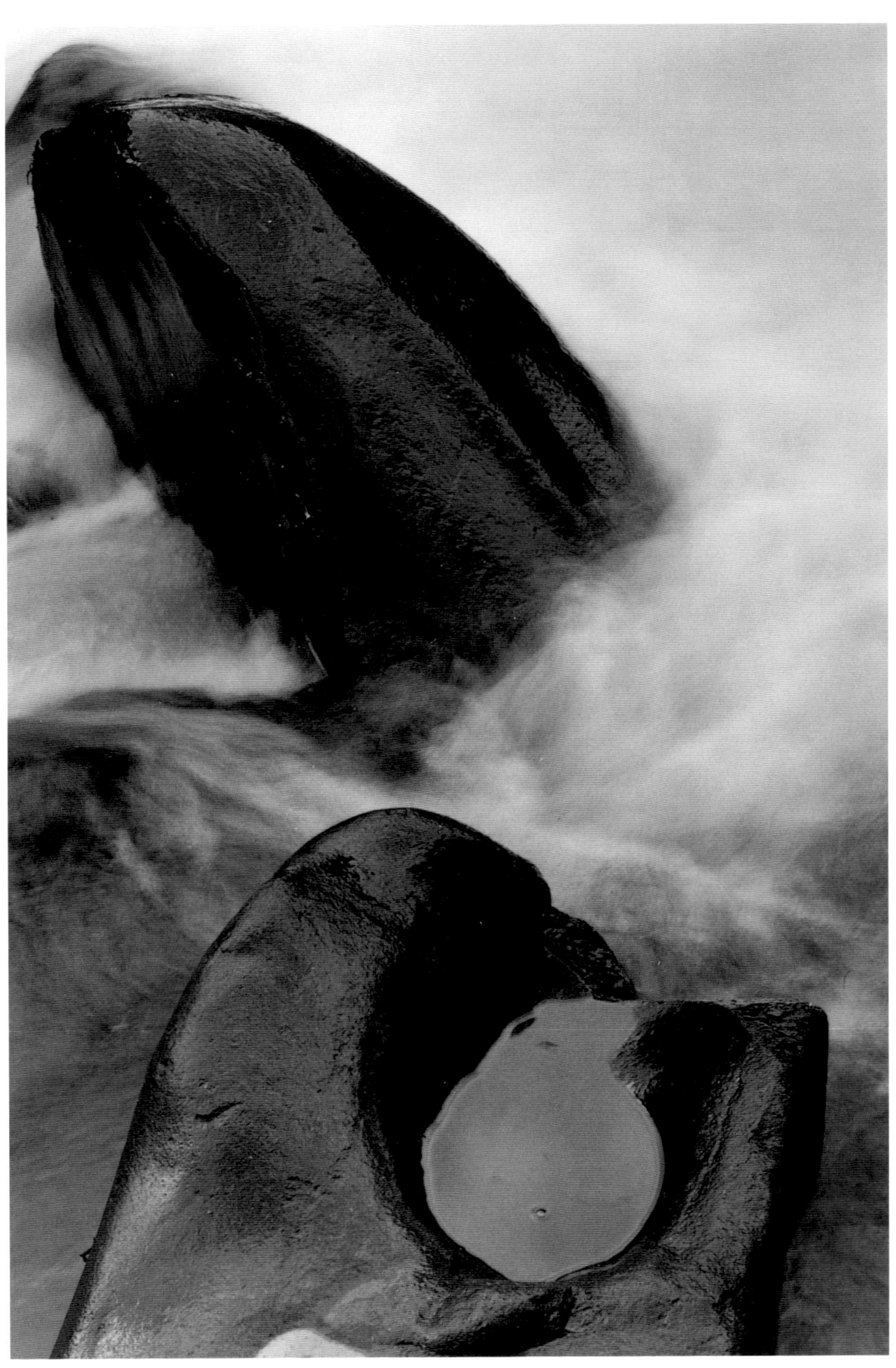

Farmer

North Carolina

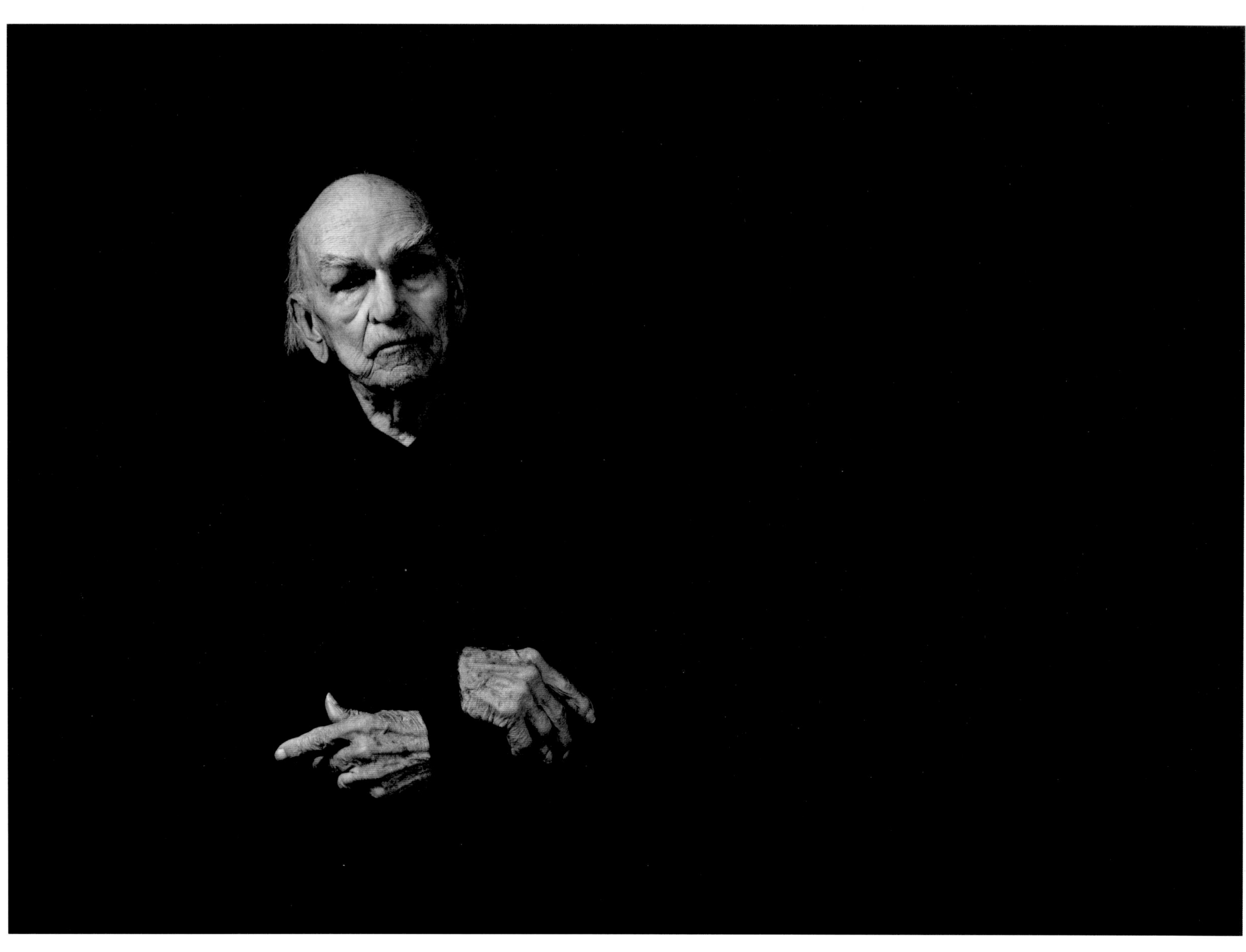

Lost in Translation
Durham, North Carolina

Elizabeth Matheson

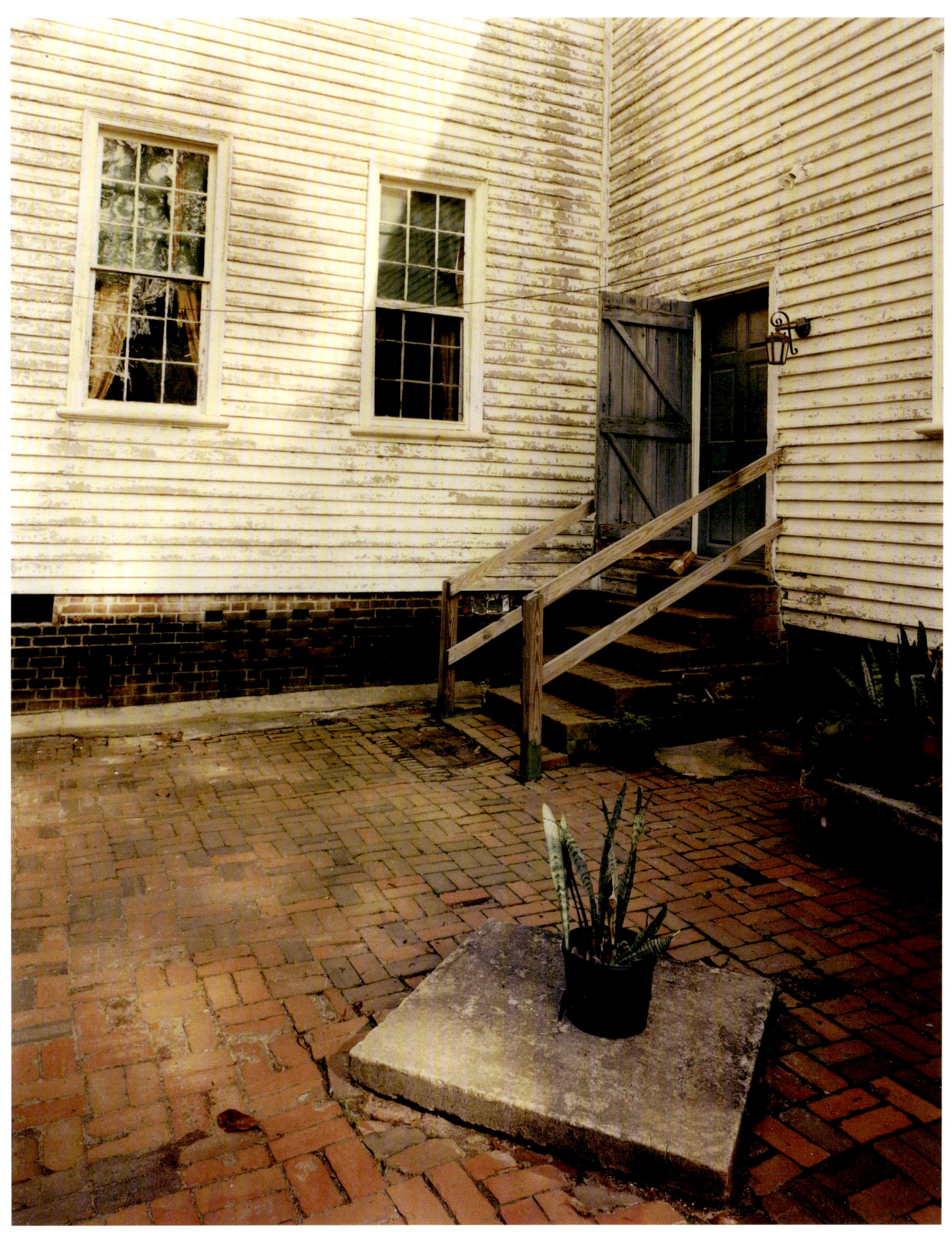

Shell Castle

Enfield, North Carolina

Shell Castle
Enfield, North Carolina

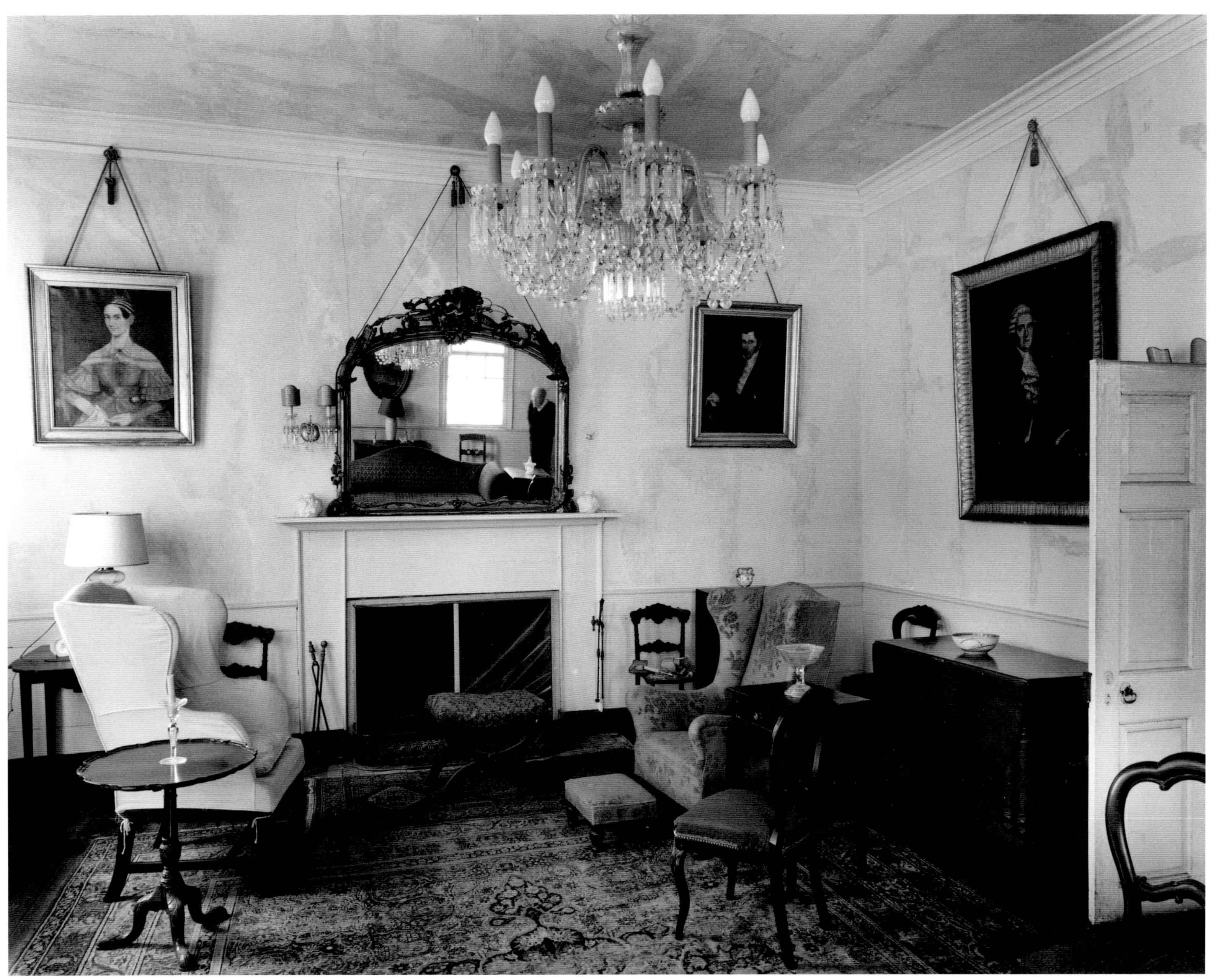

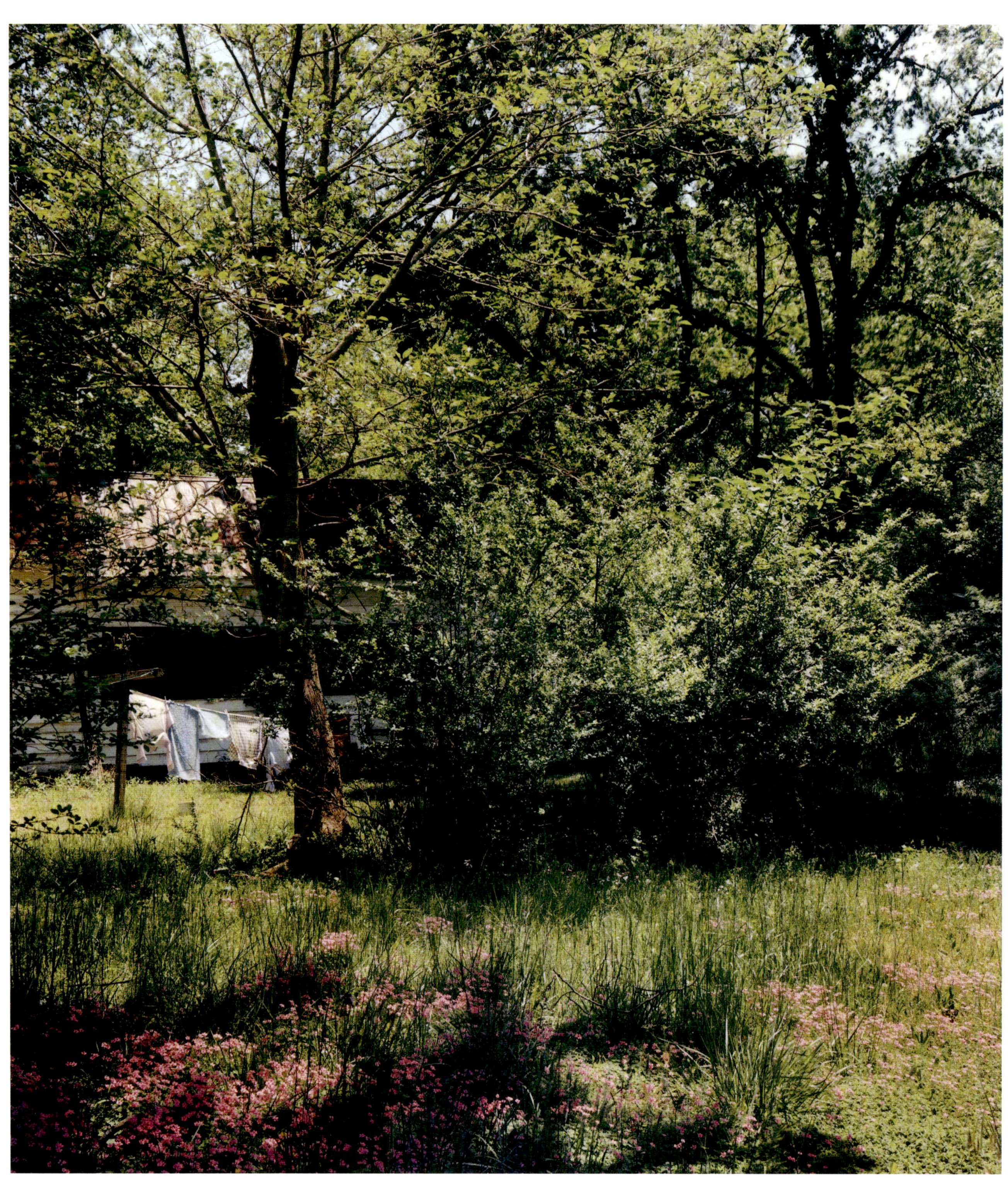

Shell Castle
Enfield, North Carolina

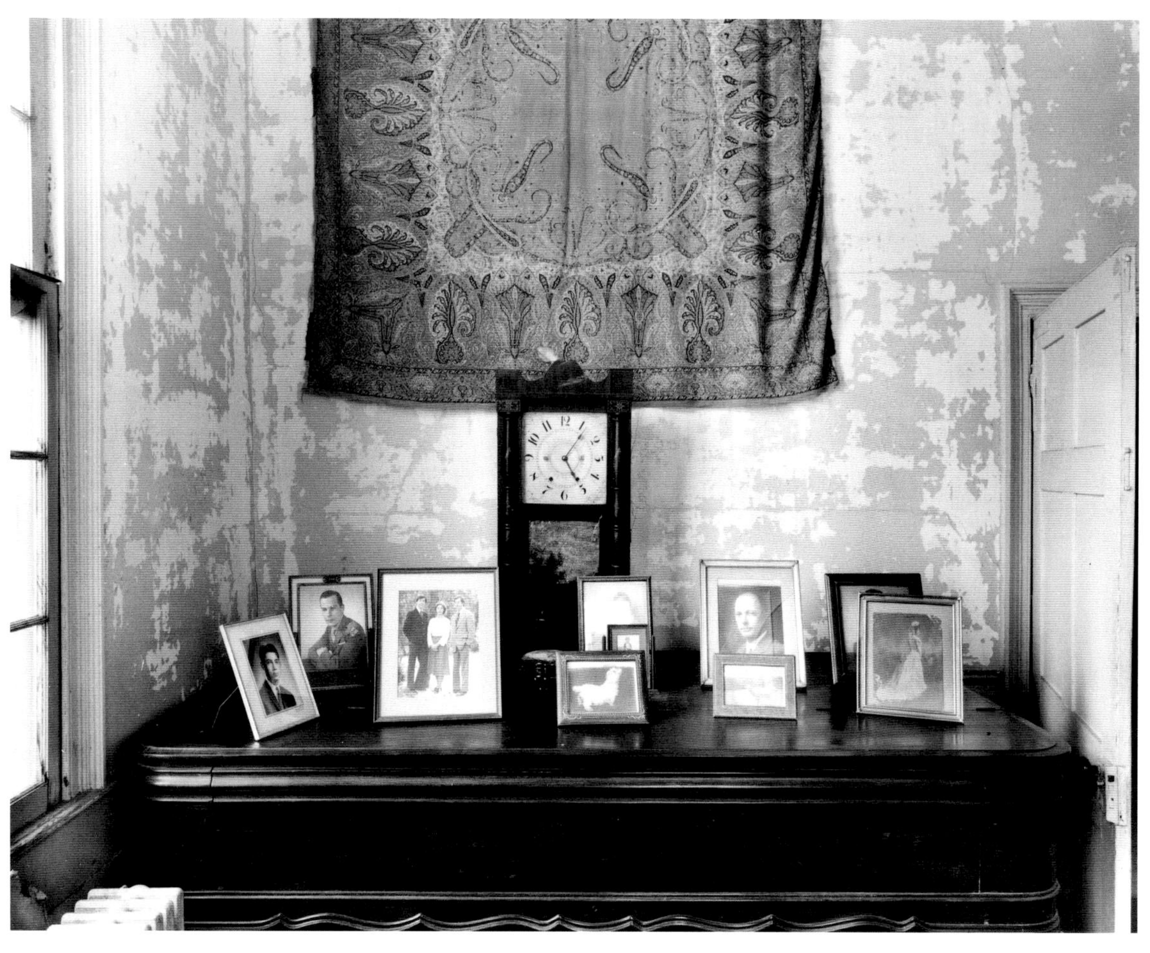

Shell Castle
Enfield, North Carolina

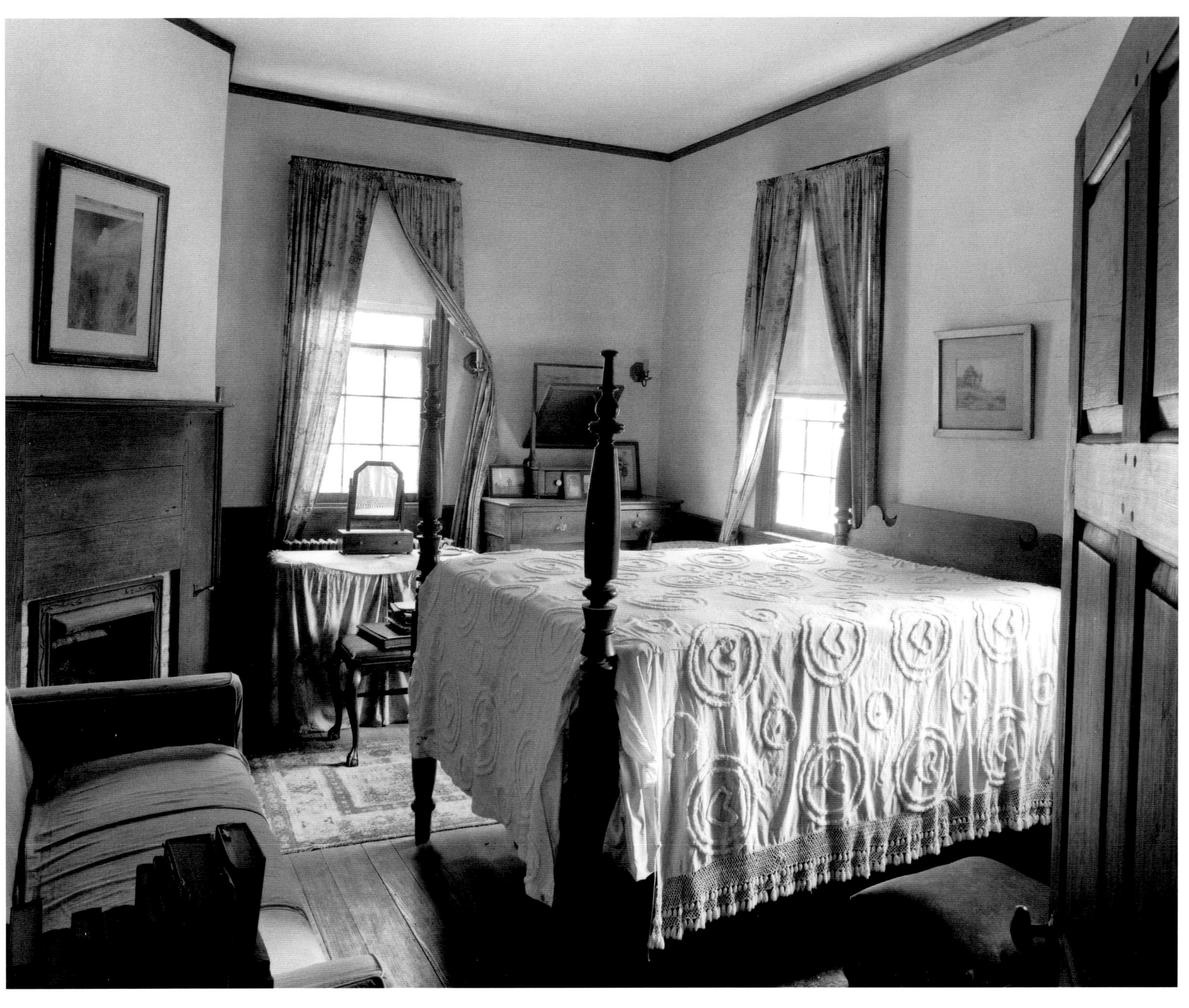

Shell Castle

Enfield, North Carolina

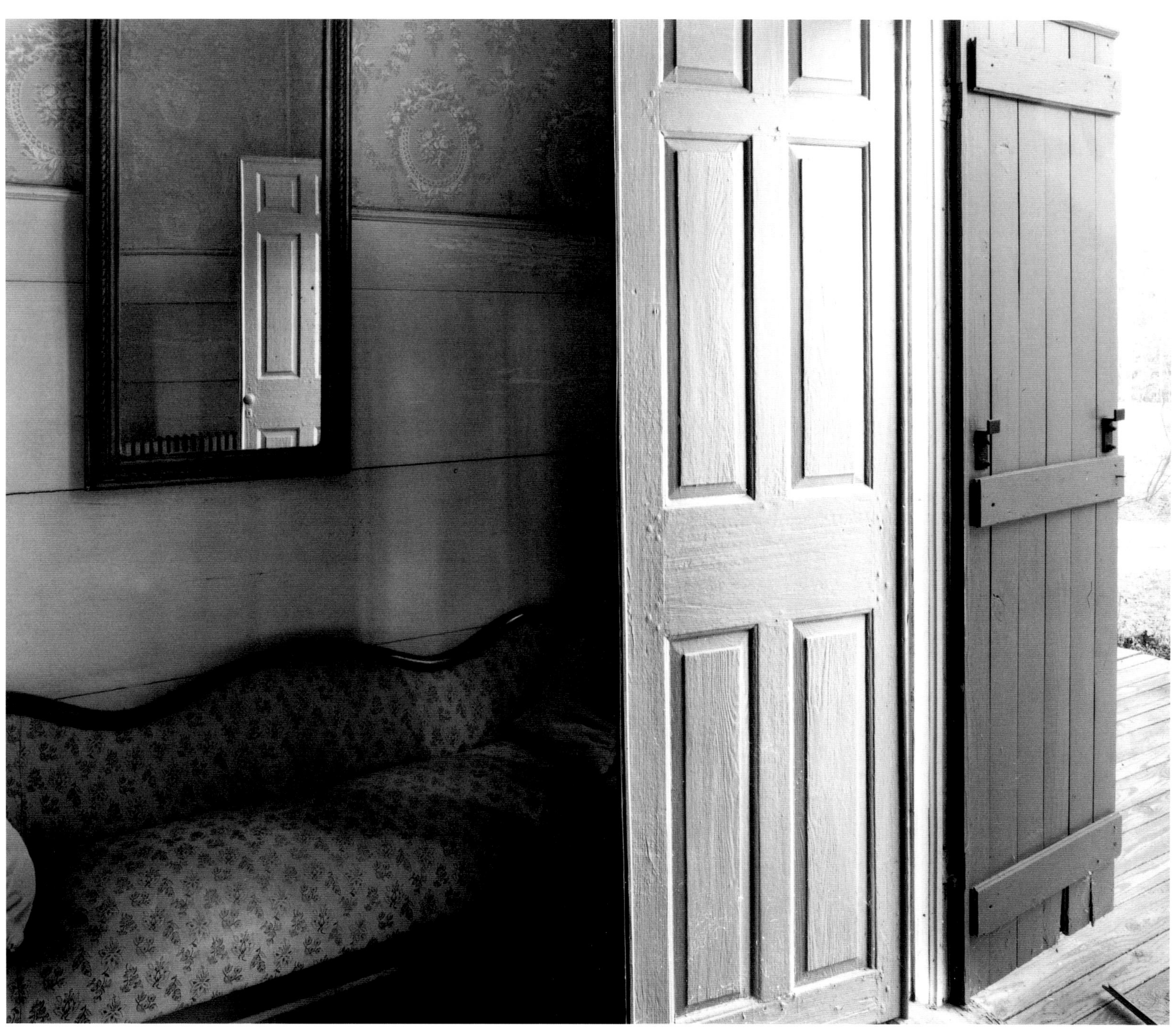

Shell Castle

Enfield, North Carolina

South Beach
Miami, Florida

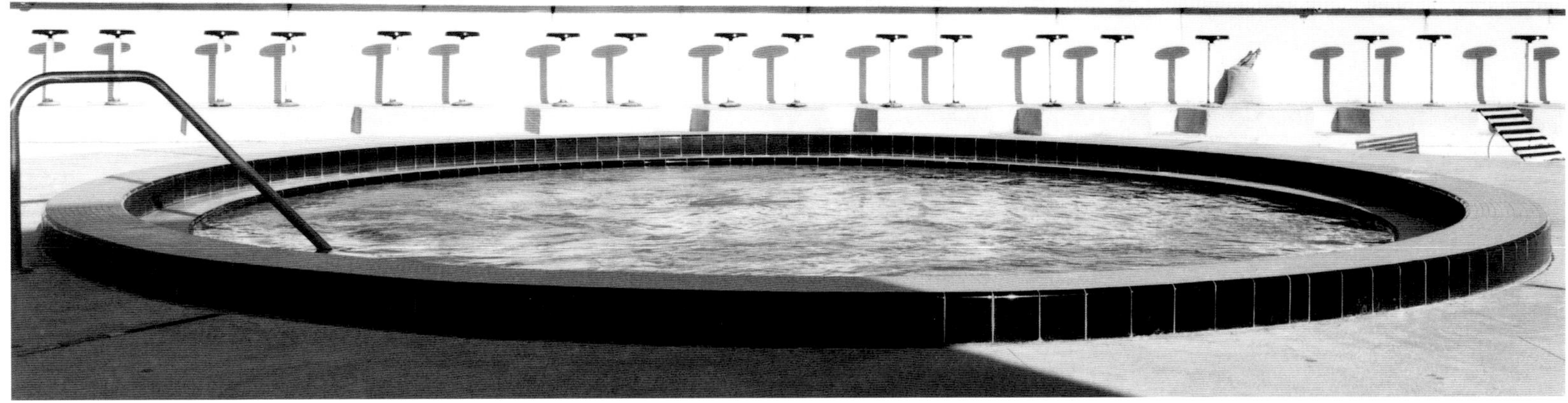

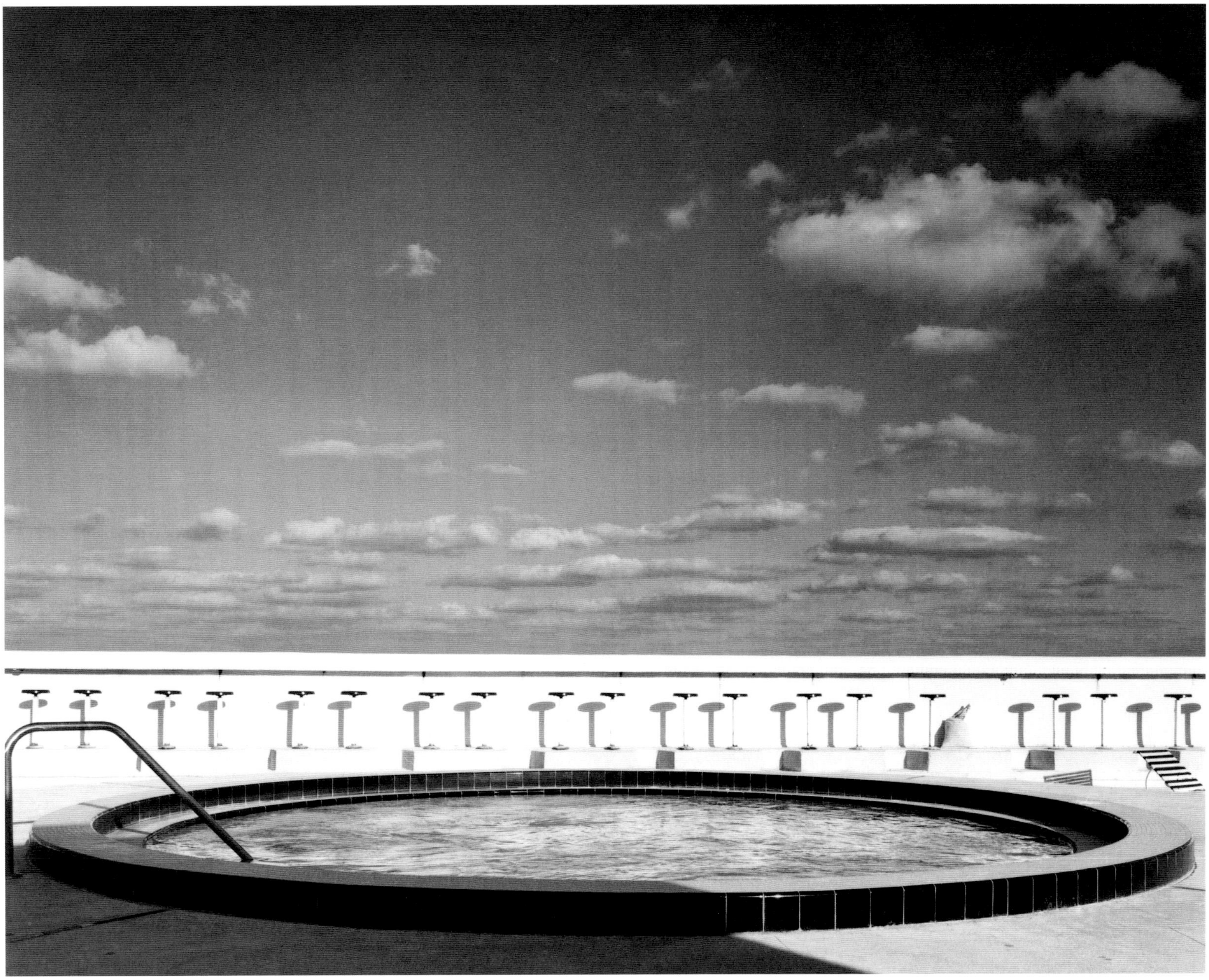

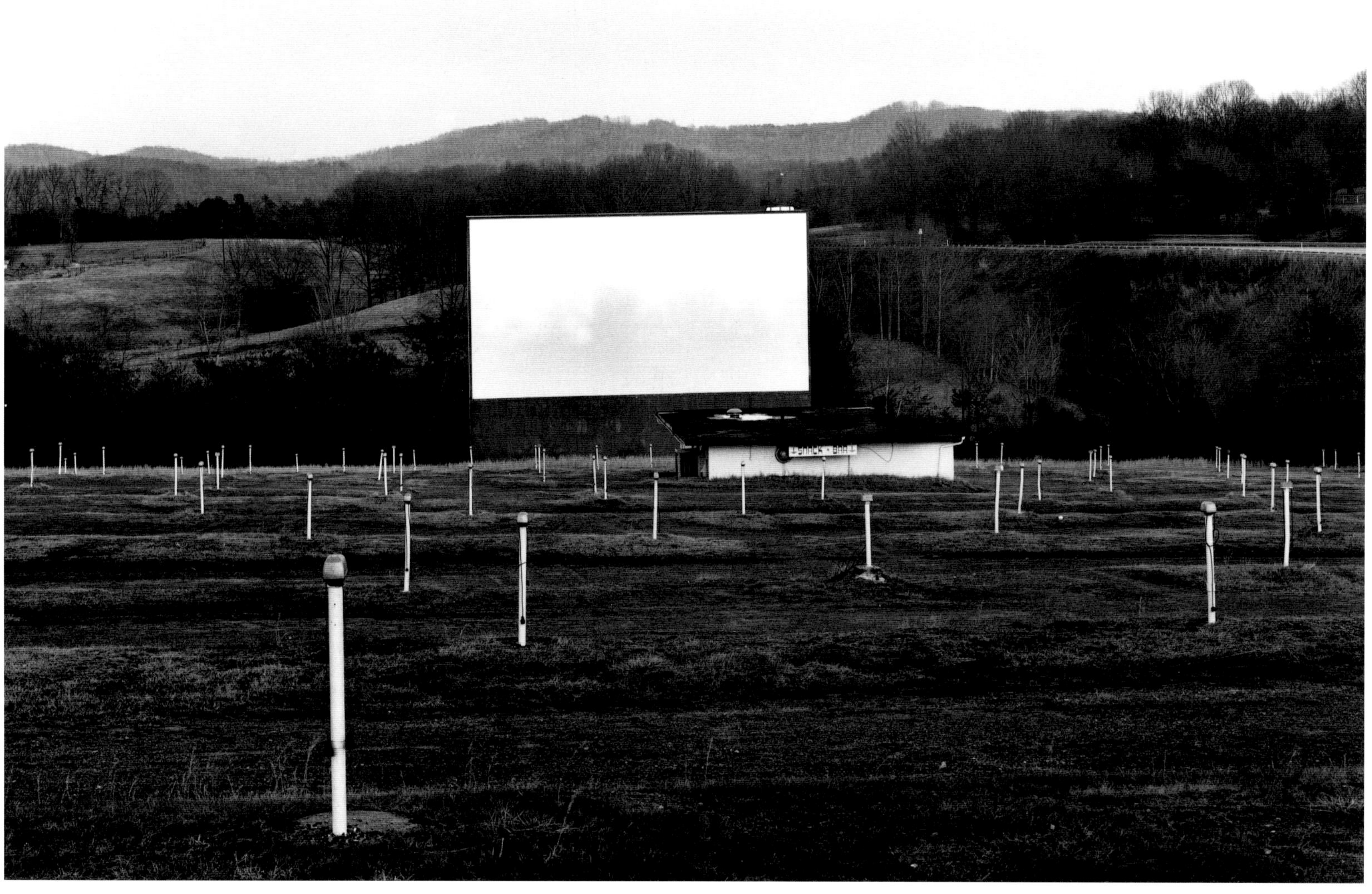

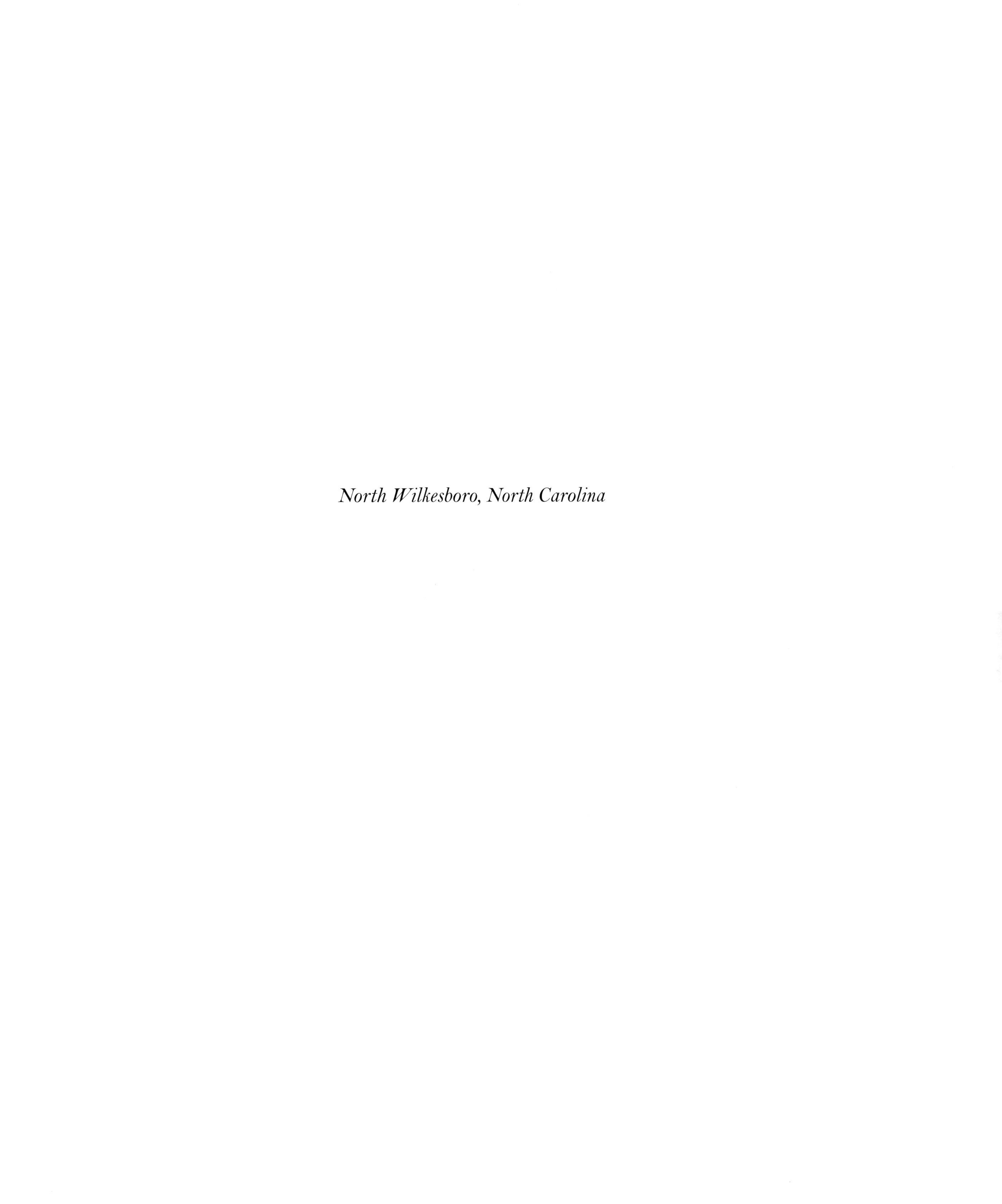

North Wilkesboro, North Carolina

John Rosenthal

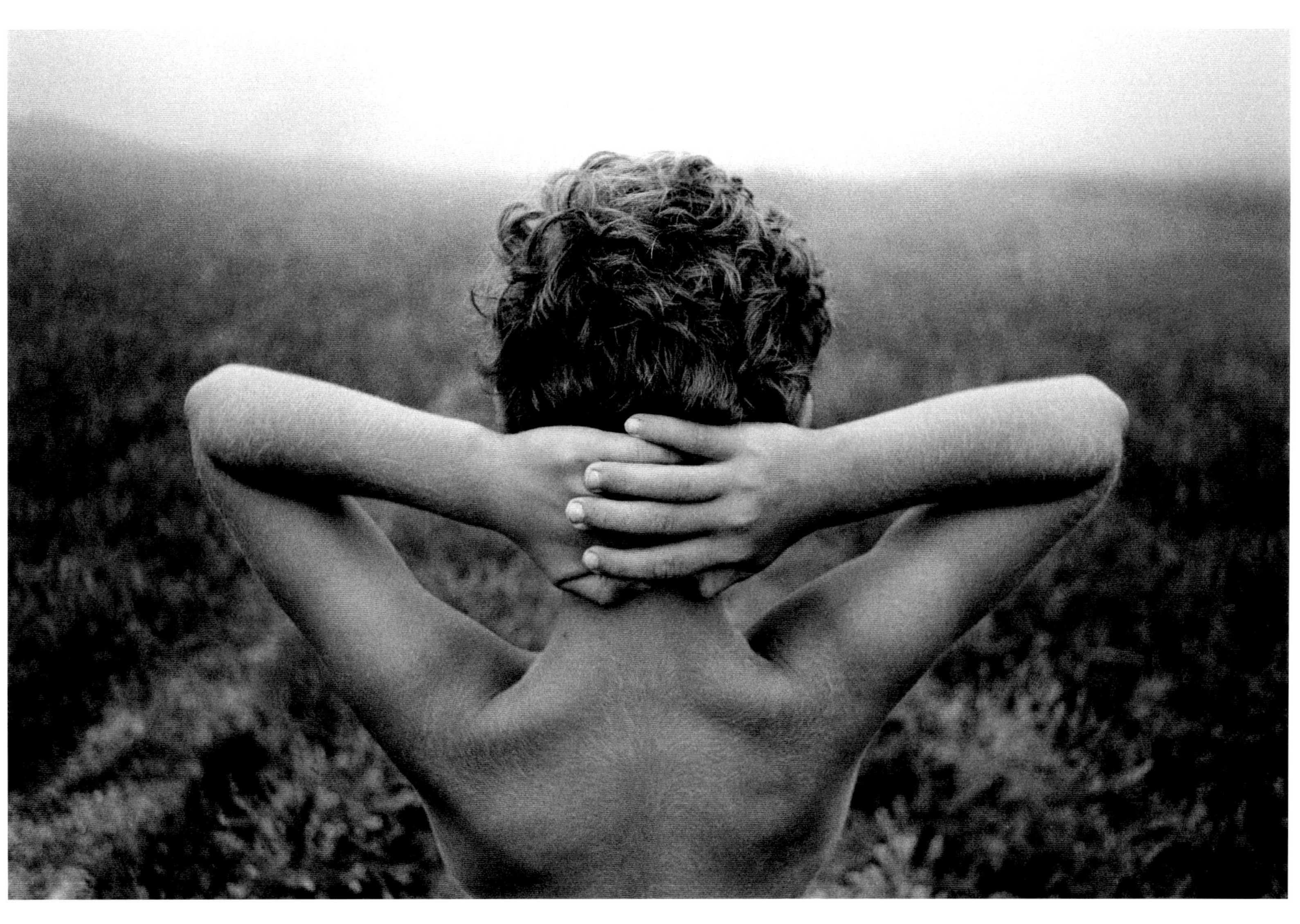

John Keats Rosenthal
Valle Crucis, North Carolina

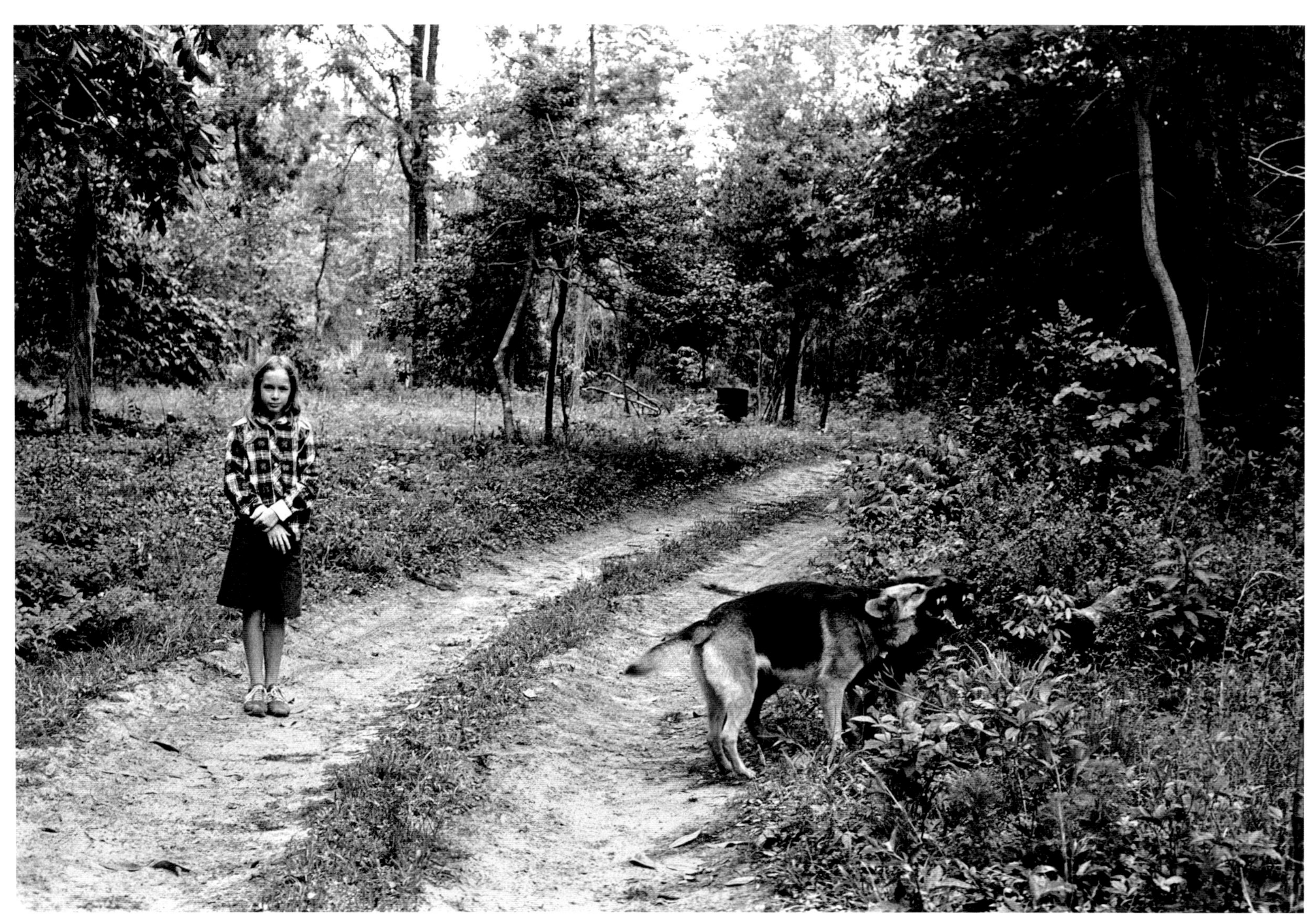

Lydia
Wrightsville Beach, North Carolina

Cat

Chapel Hill, North Carolina

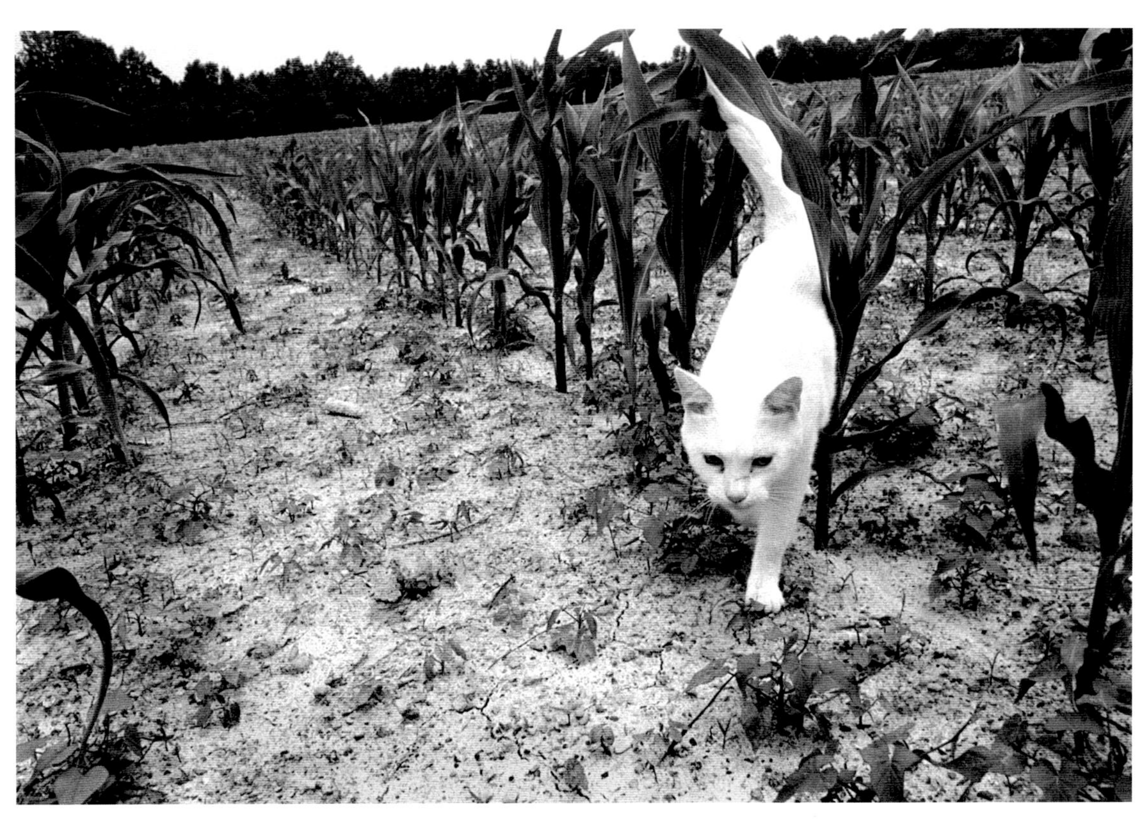

Hippos, National Zoo
Washington, D.C.

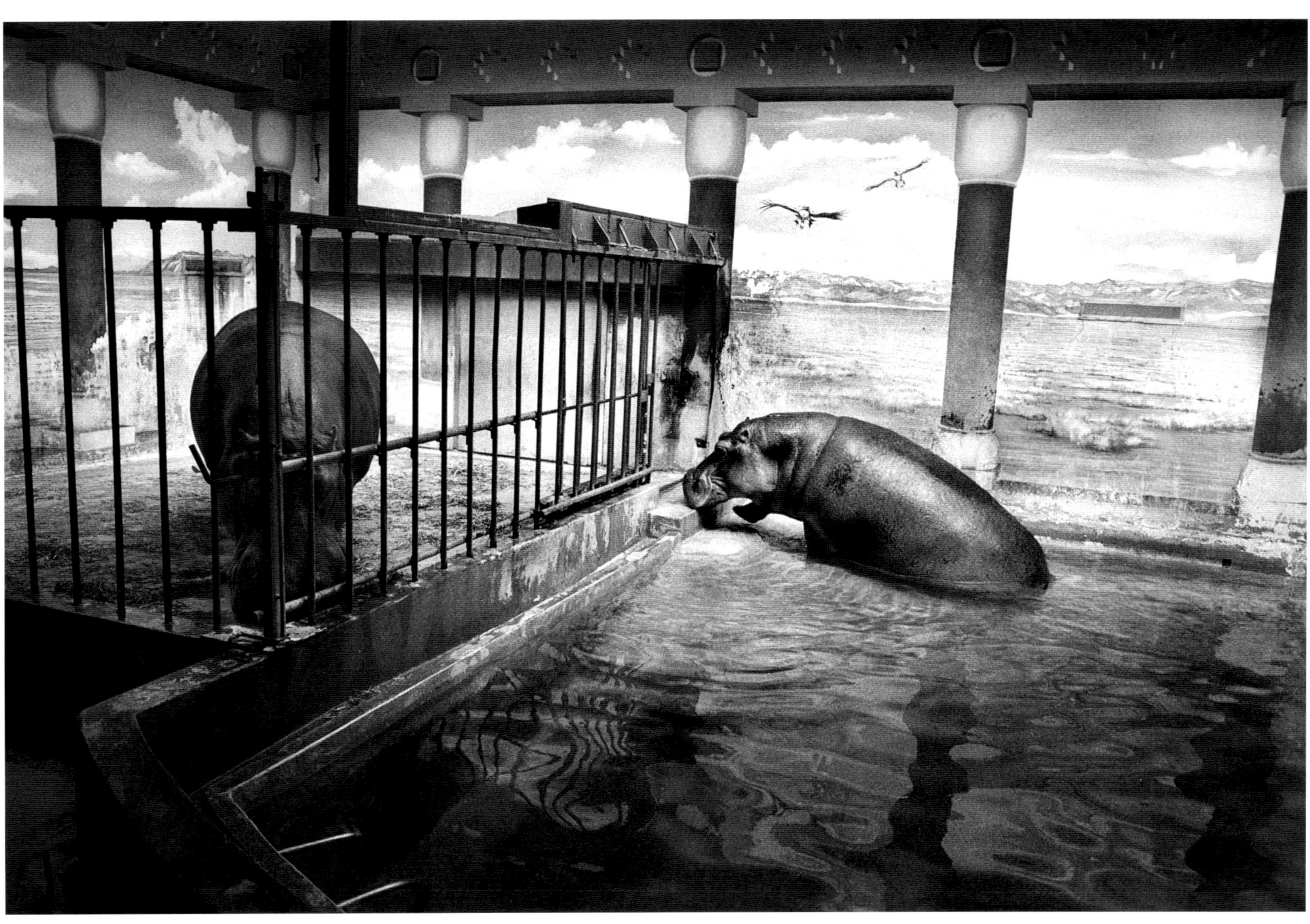

Statue of Liberty
Lake Worth, Florida

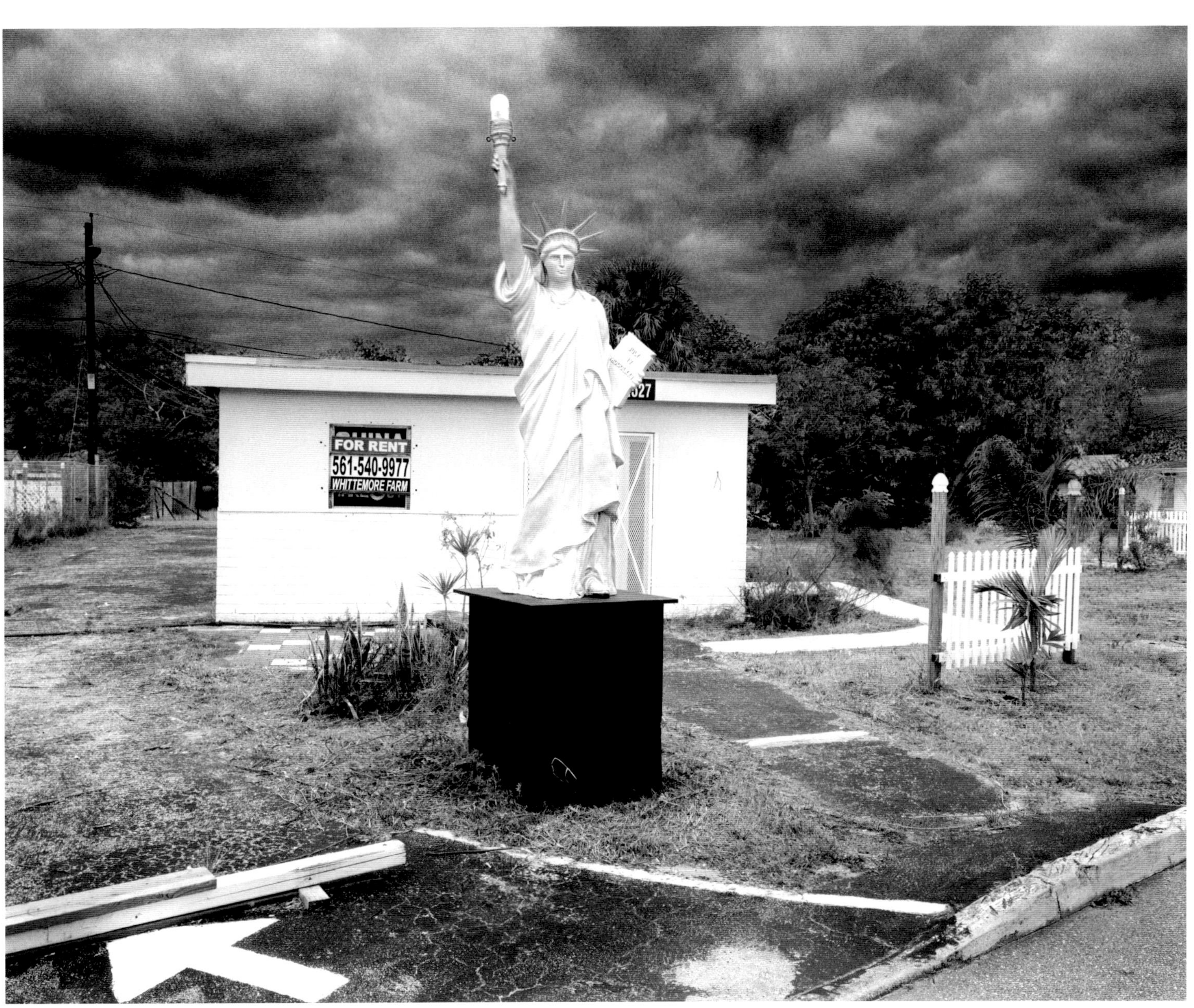

FOR RENT
561·540·9977
WHITTEMORE FARM

Sunbathers

Carolina Beach, North Carolina

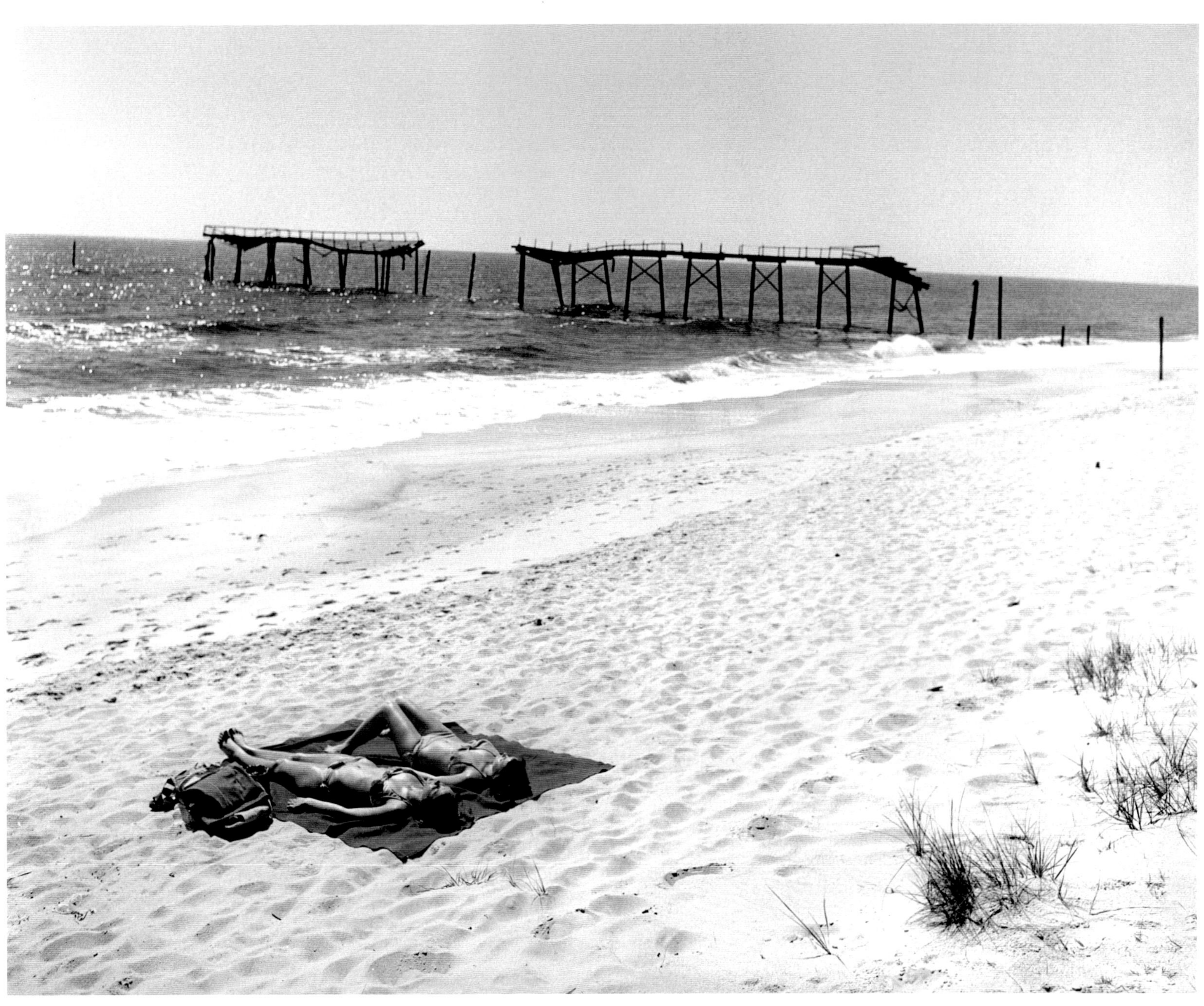

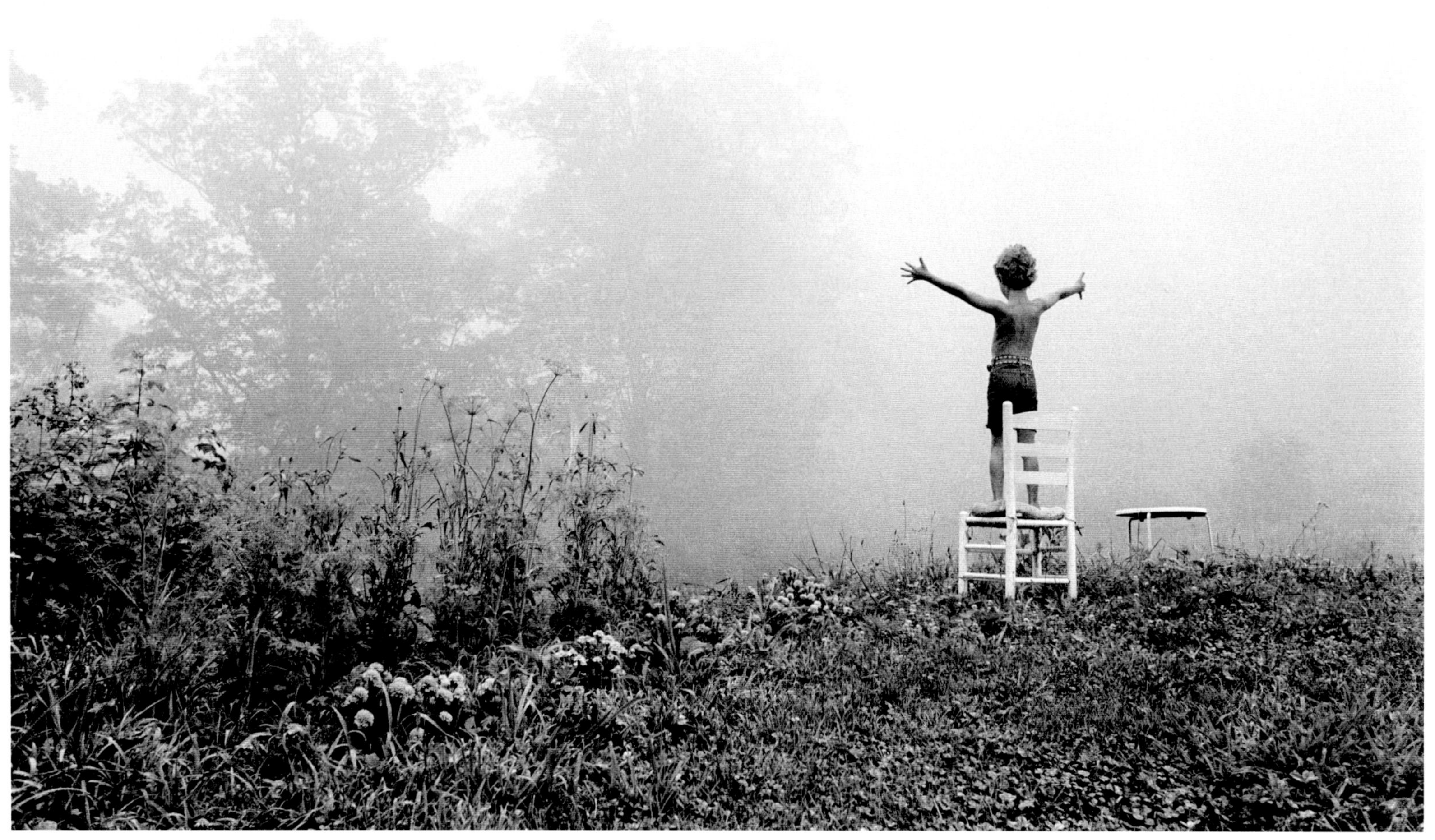

John Keats Rosenthal

Valle Crucis, North Carolina

Bar

Venice, California

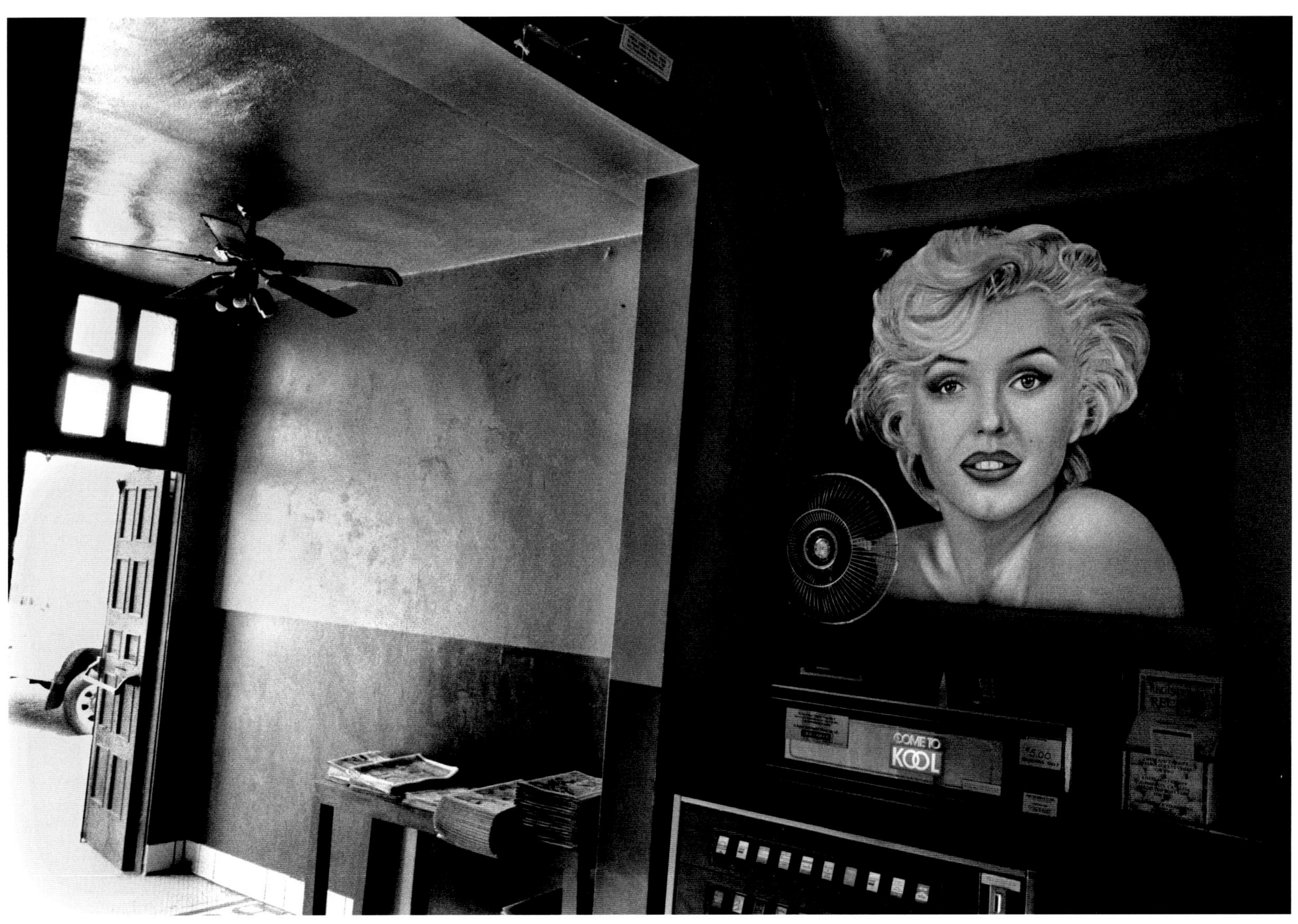

COME TO
KOOL

Andrew Bellamy, Pine Forest Cemetery

Wilmington, North Carolina

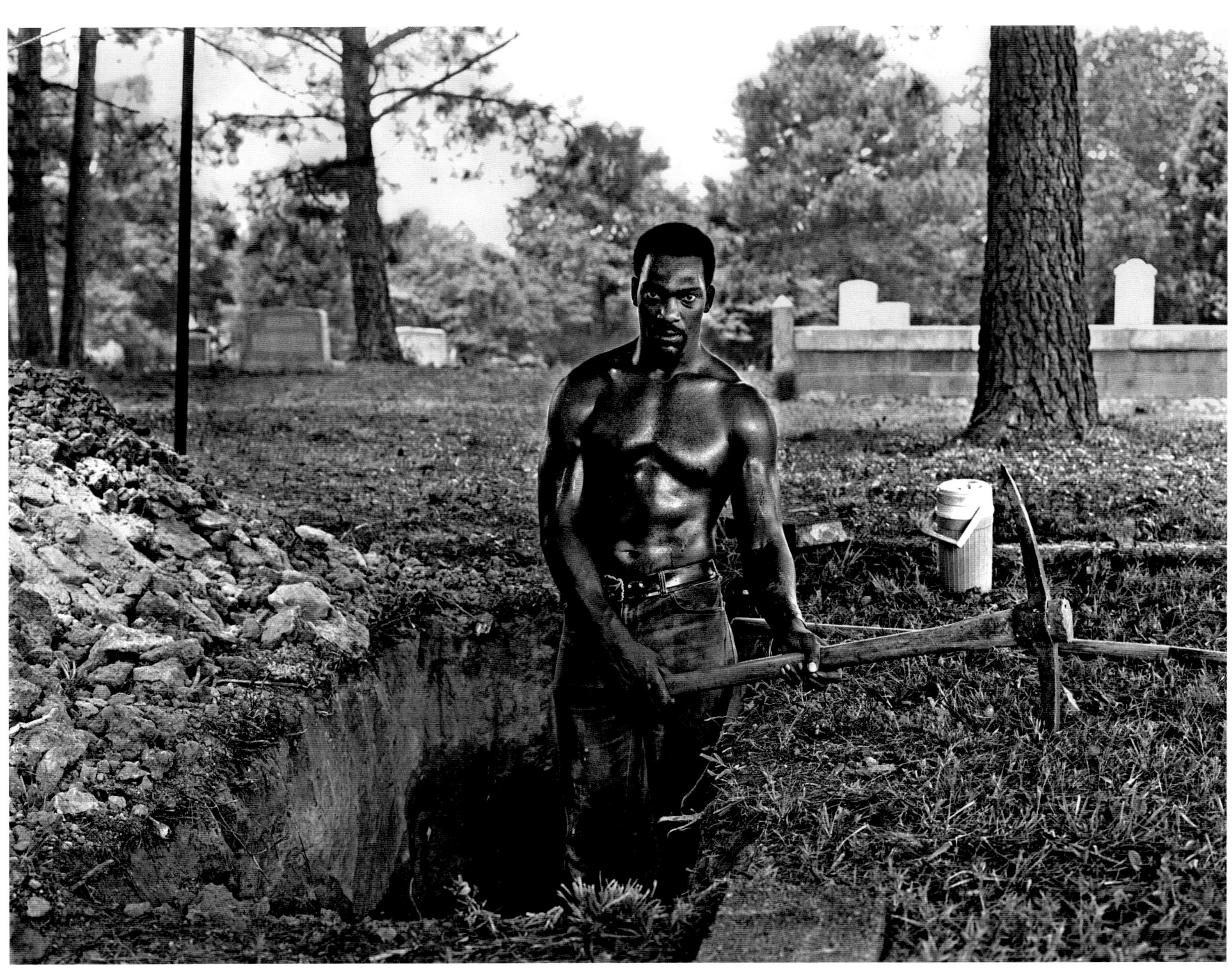

About the Artists

Rob Amberg's photographs and writings from the rural South have been published and exhibited nationally and internationally in numerous journals, magazines, and galleries. He frequently lectures and does assignment work for non-profit organizations, philanthropic foundations, and editorial publications. He has received fellowships and awards from the National Endowment for the Humanities, the John Simon Guggenheim Foundation, the Center for Documentary Studies, Alternative Roots, and the National Endowment for the Arts. His book, *Sodom Laurel Album*, published in 2002 by the University of North Carolina Press and the Center for Documentary Studies at Duke University, won the 2003 Thomas Wolfe Memorial Literary Award from the Western Carolina Historical Association. He is currently working on a book documenting a nine-mile section of interstate highway recently opened in mountainous Madison County, North Carolina, where he lives with his wife, two children, and an assortment of animals.

Caroline Vaughan was educated at Duke University and later studied with John Menapace at the Penland School of Crafts. She was one of only seven students in a graduate seminar at MIT with master photographer Minor White. Soon thereafter, Ms. Vaughan was nominated by a panel of photographic experts from Europe, North America, and Australia as one of forty-three promising young photographers listed in Time Life's "Photography Year" 1977 edition. Her photographs have been published in numerous magazine, including *Camera*, *Zoom*, *Aperture*, and *Parnassus: Poetry in Review*. In 1996 Duke University Press published *Borrowed Time: Photographs of Caroline Vaughan*, a midlife assessment of her work. She is included in Polaroid's comprehensive survey of its collection, the *Polaroid Book*. She has had solo exhibitions at the Amon Carter Museum, the Neikrug Gallery, the Light Factory, the Green Hill Center of North Carolina Art, and Hollins University. Among the museums that collect Ms. Vaughan's works are the Addison Gallery of American Art, the Amon Carter Museum, the Houston Museum of Fine Arts, and the North Carolina Museum of Art. The Gallery of Art and Design at North Carolina State University will archive Ms. Vaughan's photography.

Elizabeth Matheson was educated at Sweet Briar College and studied photography with John Menapace at the Penland School of Crafts. Her affection for old North Carolina towns and houses is reflected in her books on Edenton and her native Hillsborough (with Jerry Eidenier). Other books include *To See* with poems of John McFee (Wesleyan University Press, 1991) and *Blithe Air: Photographs of England, Wales, and Ireland* (Jargon Society Press, 1995). She has had solo exhibitions at Virginia Polytechnic Institute, Hollins University, Western Carolina University, the North Carolina Museum of Art, the National Humanities Center, and, most recently, the Gallery of Art and Design at North Carolina State University. In 2003 she was included in the Ackland Art Museum's "Defining Moments, Two Centuries of Photography." In 2004 she received the North Carolina Governor's Award in Fine Arts.

John Rosenthal's photographs have been exhibited throughout North Carolina and the Southeast. His one-person shows include exhibits at the National Humanities Center, the Asheville Museum of Art, the National Academy of Sciences, the NIH, and the Green Hill Center for North Carolina Art, as well as Wake Forest University, Elon University, Salem College, Hollins University, and the School of Design at North Carolina State University. His essays and photography have appeared in various journals and periodicals, including *ARTVU, Five Points, Carolina Quarterly, Sun Magazine, Key West Review, Kenyon Review, NCArts, New York Magazine, Arts Journal,* and *In Brief, Short Takes on the Personal.* Mr. Rosenthal has written and lectured widely on his own work and the work of others, including presentations at the City Gallery of Contemporary Art, the Weatherspoon Art Gallery, and the North Carolina Museum of Art. He has served as a visiting lecturer at Duke University's Institute of the Arts. In 2003 Mr. Rosenthal provided the narration and eighty-five photographs for the *Morrison Project,* winner of the Best Documentary at the 2003 Hamptons International Film Festival. In 1985 Mr. Rosenthal began his career as a radio commentator on WUNC-FM, an affiliate of NPR. In 1990 he joined the roster of commentators on *All Things Considered.* In 1998 Safe Harbor Books published Mr. Rosenthal's collection *Regarding Manhattan.*

QUARTET

was designed and typeset in Bell types by
Dean Bornstein at The Perpetua Press
Peacham, Vermont

Printed in an edition of 1,000 copies by
Meridian Printing Company
East Greenwich, Rhode Island

Bound at Acme Bookbinding
Charlestown, Massachusetts